SOLVING

Unraveling the Perplexing and

BIBLE

Troubling Passages of Scripture

MYSTERIES

D. JAMES KENNEDY

A JANET THOMA BOOK

THOMAS NELSON PUBLISHERS®
Nashville

Published in Nashville, Tennessee, by Thomas Nelson, Inc.

Unless otherwise noted, Scripture quotations are from THE KING JAMES VERSION.

Scripture quotations noted NKJV are from THE NEW KING JAMES VERSION. Copyright © 1979, 1980, 1982 Thomas Nelson, Inc., Publishers.

All quotations from the Sherlock Holmes stories of Sir Arthur Conan Doyle are in the public domain and were electronically retrieved from the Project Gutenberg Web site at http://www.gutenberg.net/.

ISBN 0-7852-7041-8

Printed in the United States of America

1 2 3 4 5 6 BVG 05 04 03 02 01 00

This book is affectionately dedicated to all future readers who are apparently perplexed by some of the mysteries contained in the Bible. My wish and prayer is that through the pages of this book, many of those mysteries will be solved, meanings will become plain, and readers will discover that in spite of apparent confusion, it is, "after all, elementary, my dear Watson."

CONTENTS

Acknowledgments   vii

Introduction: I Love a Mystery!   ix

Part I
Mysteries That Trouble the Soul

Mystery 1: Can a Christian Fall from Grace?   3

Mystery 2: Is It Possible Not to Sin?   14

Mystery 3: Which Is True–Predestination or Free Will?   23

Mystery 4: Should We Judge or Not Judge?   32

Part II
Mysteries of the Gospel Story

Mystery 5: The Mystery of the Virgin Birth   47

Mystery 6: More Mysteries of the Birth of Christ
   Genealogies and Prophecies   61

Mystery 7: Mysteries of the Death and Resurrection
   of Christ   74

Contents

Part III
Mysteries of the Creation, Fall, and Flood

Mystery 8: Doesn't the Genesis Creation Story
Contradict Science?   97

Mystery 9: Doesn't the Book of Genesis Contradict Itself?   116

Part IV
Mysteries of the Nature of God

Mystery 10: The Mystery of the Incarnation
Is Jesus God or the Son of God?   129

Mystery 11: The Mystery of the Trinity
How Can God Be Both *Three* and *One*?   149

Part V
The Mystery of Our Salvation

Mystery 12: How Can a Loving God Send People to Hell?   165

Mystery 13: Are We Saved by Faith or Works?   188

Notes   208

About the Author   211

ACKNOWLEDGMENTS

I wish to express my appreciation to Jim Denney, who fashioned the material into the shape found in this book; to Dan Scalf, who worked with the publishers to make the book possible; to Nancy Britt, who edited the manuscript; and to my executive assistant, Mary Anne Bunker, who did the final edit.

And He said, "Unto you it is given to know the mysteries of the kingdom of God."

Luke 8:10

"I confess that I can make neither head nor tail of it. Don't you think that you have kept up your mystery long enough, Mr. Holmes?"

"Certainly, Colonel, you shall know everything."

Sir Arthur Conan Doyle
"Silver Blaze"

I LOVE A MYSTERY!

*It was on a bitterly cold and frosty morning, towards the end of
the winter of '97, that I was awakened by a tugging at my shoulder. It was Holmes. The candle in his hand shone upon his eager,
stooping face, and told me at a glance that something was amiss.
"Come, Watson, come!" he cried. "The game is afoot!"*

So begins one of Sir Arthur Conan Doyle's most famous Sherlock
Holmes mysteries, "The Adventure of the Abbey Grange."

I love a good mystery! Don't you? We feel a thrill in the soul and a
tingle in the spine as we follow the master sleuth, Sherlock Holmes,
into yet another perilous and baffling adventure. We feel awe as we
watch him make shrewd, profound deductions from the scantiest of
clues. Once the mystery is solved, we feel a sense of deep satisfaction
and relief.

But what about a *real-life* mystery? You and I are not fictional
detectives. We are ordinary people facing the ordinary problems and
pressures of life. When we are forced to confront the perplexity and
confusion of a mystery—well, that's not nearly as much fun as watching Sherlock Holmes solve a fictional crime.

When we approach God's Word, we are sometimes puzzled and
perplexed. We encounter statements we cannot comprehend, seemingly conflictive narratives, and principles that seem to clash with

principles found elsewhere in Scripture. Sometimes these Bible mysteries become a source of doubt in our own inner being.

At other times, when we seek to share the truth of God's Word with friends, some skeptic sneers, "You don't really believe that stuff, do you? Everyone knows the Bible is full of errors and contradictions!"

The world is full of scoffers, atheists, secularists, and humanists who enjoy nothing better than ridiculing and mocking the Christian faith. One enterprising group even went so far as to publish a series of anti-evangelistic flash cards that unbelievers can use whenever someone tries to share the Gospel with them. These colorful laminated cards are called "Bible-Thumper Stumpers," and they cite chapter-and-verse Bible references that are supposedly contradictory. The purpose of these Bible-Thumper Stumper cards, say the publishers, is to either send Christians fleeing or to cause Christians to doubt their own faith.

Hence this book. I have written *Solving Bible Mysteries* because I know there are forces out there—not only anti-Christian people and organizations, but malevolent *spiritual* forces—that seek to destroy your faith. These forces will use anything—even the seeming mysteries in God's own Word—as a wedge between your soul and a trusting faith in God. I want you to be fully prepared with the truth whenever your faith is under attack. As the Scriptures tell us, "Be ready always to give an answer to every man that asketh you a reason of the hope that is in you"(1 Peter 3:15).

The good news about Bible mysteries is that they are all solvable—and most of them are solved much more easily than you might think. Often, problems in understanding God's Word are the result of difficulties that arise when Hebrew or Greek concepts are translated into English. Other problems are solved when we discover that so-called conflicting biblical principles actually complement each other to give a more complete picture of spiritual truth. Supposed contradictions between Bible narratives (such as different Gospel accounts of the same event) are often nothing more than differences in the selection of details to include or omit.

I believe your faith will be strengthened and magnified as we go sleuthing for solutions to these Bible mysteries. Along our journey together, you will begin to see that Christianity is not a blind faith, but a *reasonable* and *informed* faith, based on historical facts that can be confirmed. You will see that the truth of God's Word always stands up under questioning and scrutiny. You will be equipped and ready to give a defense of the hope that is in you, so that you won't be stumped by such questions as:

- Can a Christian lose his salvation?

- Which is true—predestination or free will?

- Do Genesis 1 and 2 offer contradictory accounts of creation?

- Where did Cain get his wife?

- Doesn't the Bible violate modern scientific knowledge?

- Aren't there contradictions in the story of Noah and the ark?

- Don't the Matthew and Luke genealogies of Jesus contradict each other?

- Why does the Bible tell us to judge—and to judge not?

- How could Jesus have been in the tomb for three full days if He was crucified on Friday and rose on Sunday?

- Don't the two accounts of Judas's death contradict each other?

- Are we saved by faith or by works, as James 2 seems to say?

- How can a loving God send people to Hell?

Be assured, there are sound, logical, well-supported answers for each of these Bible mysteries—and many more. So join me, my friend, on a grand adventure! Turn the page and explore the mysteries! Come! The game is afoot!

Part I

MYSTERIES THAT TROUBLE THE SOUL

Great is the mystery of godliness.

1 Timothy 3:16

"Well, Watson," said Holmes when our visitor had left us, "what do you make of it all?"

"I make nothing of it," I answered frankly. "It is a most mysterious business."

Sir Arthur Conan Doyle
"The Red-Headed League"

Mystery 1

CAN A CHRISTIAN FALL FROM GRACE?

Some years ago I had the privilege of sharing the Gospel with a man, and he responded by accepting Jesus Christ as his Lord and Savior. After we had prayed together, I congratulated him on the all-important step he had made in committing his life to Christ and receiving the gift of eternal life.

"Well," he said, "I just hope I'm still a Christian six months from now."

This man, who had only been a Christian for a matter of seconds, put his finger on a question that troubles many believers today: Can a Christian ever *cease* to be a Christian? Can a person who has been saved become lost once more? Can someone who has received the gift of eternal life spend eternity in Hell?

That is the Bible mystery we shall now explore.

Many Christians would say, "That is no mystery! A Christian cannot lose his salvation! Once saved, always saved! We are kept by the power of God unto the salvation that is ready to be revealed in the last days, as the Bible says."

But many sincere, Bible-believing Christians have a very different perspective on this mystery. They say, "Yes, it is possible to lose your faith, your salvation, and your position in God's grace. In fact, it has

3

happened many times." And they proceed to point out the many people who have made a profession of faith, been baptized, joined the church, been actively involved in the church, and perhaps even been ministers—and then they have fallen away.

In my forty-odd years of ministry, I have seen numerous people follow that course—from profession to church involvement to a tragic falling away. Often, this happened because someone in the church offended them. They would get angry and say, "Well, if that's the way things are in this church, I'm not coming back!" And they would abandon God's Church altogether.

Another phenomenon seems to suggest that Christians can lose their salvation. In some churches, Christians seem to fall away from grace every Saturday night, then get saved all over again on Sunday morning. They seem to fall out of grace, jump back in again, out, in, out, in, bound for Heaven, bound for Hell, in a never-ending cycle.

We look at such anecdotal evidence, and it truly seems that Christians can indeed lose their salvation and fall from grace. And we have to wonder: Were those people truly Christians who ceased to be Christians—or were they never truly Christians in the first place?

DID JUDAS FALL FROM GRACE?

Those who believe it is possible to lose your salvation often cite Judas Iscariot, one of the twelve apostles. He was, in fact, one of the most respected and trusted of the twelve, because they chose him to be their treasurer. He was viewed as a man of faith and integrity. Yet Judas ultimately betrayed Jesus, then went away and committed suicide. As Acts 1:25 states, Judas fell by transgression "that he might go to his own place" into everlasting condemnation. So the question is: Was Judas a Christian who fell, or was he never truly a Christian at all?

In answer to this question, we have specific revelation about Judas from Christ Himself. Early in His ministry, Jesus said, "Have not I chosen you twelve, and one of you is a devil?" (John 6:70) Put this together with the fact that Judas went "to his own place" when he hanged himself, and I think the status of Judas becomes clear. He manifested what Christ said he would manifest. Judas was a "devil" when Christ chose him; he was a "devil" when he walked with Christ, carrying the treasury of the disciples; he was a "devil" when he betrayed the innocent blood of Christ; and he was a "devil" when he died and went "to his own place." Judas did not fall from grace. He never partook of grace in the first place.

We also have the Word of God as witness that those who abandon the Church and Christ were never really saved. First John 2:19 says: "They went out from us, but they were not of us; for if they had been of us, they would no doubt have continued with us: but they went out, that they might be made manifest that they were not all of us."

Here again, we see the Word of God describing people who left but who did not fall from grace. The truth is that they were never partakers of grace in the first place. We cannot tell by looking at a person if he or she is a genuine Christian; our powers of observation are not infallible. But the revelation of God tells us that those who fall away were never part of us to begin with, and the revelation of God is always infallibly true.

Is it possible for a person to accept Christ, be baptized, join a church, then live forty or fifty years in sin, serving the devil rather than God, and then die and go to Heaven? I have never seen such a scenario revealed in Scripture.

Then does the Bible say that a person can become saved, serve God for a lifetime, commit one terrible sin, then die and go to Hell? No, I've never seen that in Scripture either.

What *do* we find in Scripture? We see that genuine Christians may *temporarily* and *partially* fall away, but they will inevitably come back. The great example is Peter, who denied Christ three times. Yet, when Jesus confronted Peter, he returned to Christ in a broken and repentant state. The difference between Judas and Peter is that Peter came back to Christ.

THE PERSEVERANCE OF THE SAINTS

One theological term that describes the doctrine of "once saved, always saved" is *the perseverance of the saints*. To understand what that means, we need to understand what a saint is. Many people think of a saint as a kind of a super-Christian who belongs to the Heavenly Hall of Fame. That's not what a saint is at all! Every genuine Christian is a saint. The word *saint* comes from the same root word as *sanctify*, which means "to cleanse and set aside for use." As Christians we have been sanctified—cleansed by the blood of Christ and set aside for His use. Every true Christian is sanctified and is, therefore, a saint.

What, then, is the perseverance of the saints? Some people refer to this as the doctrine of "eternal security" or the "preservation of the saints," but these terms do not convey the truest sense of the doctrine of the perseverance of the saints. The Scriptures do not talk simply in terms of security or preservation. No, the terminology of Scripture is active, not passive: *perseverance* is a dynamic and descriptive word.

The Bible is very clear that we are enabled by God to continue and to persevere unto the end. Jesus Himself said, "He that endureth to the end shall be saved" (Matt. 10:22). And again, "But he that shall endure unto the end, the same shall be saved" (Matt. 24:13). So here is a point of agreement between those who believe that people can fall away and those who believe salvation is secure and final the moment we accept Christ as Lord and Savior: Only those who persevere unto the end are saved. You cannot accept Christ, live for the devil, and then die and go to Heaven.

If both sides believe a Christian must persevere to the end in order to be saved, what is the difference between those two views? One side believes that Christians must persevere in their own strength, their own will. The other side—the view I espouse—believes that *God alone* enables us by His Spirit to continue on and persevere unto the end. Those who believe they must persevere in their own strength will usually find themselves on a spiritual seesaw: they fall and are lifted up, fall, are lifted up, and on and on. If they are fortunate enough to die on a spiritual upswing, they are saved; if they die during a fall, they go to Hell—tough luck!

You've probably seen the poster that shows a cat hanging by its claws on a tree limb with the inscription, "Hang in there, baby." Is that what your spiritual life is like? Are you just hanging in there with all of your strength? That view leaves God out of the picture. God not only enables us to hang in there, but His hand is there, holding us, keeping us from falling. And that is the great hope we have—not only that we have been saved, but that we are being *kept* and *upheld* by the power and grace of our Almighty God.

I remember an alcoholic man who had lived for years on Skid Row. He had a friend, an ex-drunkard, who had taken him to Alcoholics Anonymous numerous times. Each time he had taken the pledge and begun to follow the Twelve Steps of AA. And each time this unfortunate man slid back into his old drinking ways. Finally, when he signed the pledge to quit drinking for the fiftieth time, his sober friend said, "Now this time, *keep* the pledge!"

"Keep the pledge?" exclaimed the alcoholic. "Man, I need someone to keep *me!*"

This man describes the state of all of us. Sin is the ultimate addiction. We cannot beat it by taking a pledge. We all need to be kept by God. And thank God, we *are* "kept by the power of God through faith unto salvation ready to be revealed in the last time" (1 Peter 1:5). So we can be assured that we'll be kept by His power and grace—as long as we're sure that we are saved to begin with.

WHAT ABOUT THE WARNINGS?

A young man once came to me and asked me to explain this passage in the New Testament:

For if after they have escaped the pollutions of the world through the knowledge of the Lord and Saviour Jesus Christ, they are again entangled therein, and overcome, the latter end is worse with them than the beginning. For it had been better for them not to have known the way of righteousness, than, after they have known it, to turn from the holy commandment delivered unto them. But it is happened unto them according to the true proverb, The dog is turned to his own vomit again; and the sow that was washed to her wallowing in the mire. (2 Peter 2:20–22)

"What does that mean?" he asked.

"It means," I replied, "that if, after they have escaped the pollutions of the world through the knowledge of the Lord and Savior Jesus Christ, they are again entangled in them and overcome . . ." And I proceeded to simply recite the passage back to him, word for word.

"But," he said, surprised and chagrined, "I wanted you to *explain* what it means!"

"What is there to explain?" said I. "It means exactly what it says. There's nothing hidden or difficult to understand in that passage. It's plain and clear. What's more, other passages in Scripture say the same thing. For example, look at Hebrews 10:26–27."

We turned to that passage and read:

For if we sin wilfully after that we have received the knowledge of the truth, there remaineth no more sacrifice for sins, but a certain fearful looking for of judgment and fiery indignation, which shall devour the adversaries.

"If that hasn't convinced you," I said, "then look at this passage in Hebrews 6:4–6":

For it is impossible for those who were once enlightened, and have tasted of the heavenly gift, and were made partakers of the Holy Ghost, and have tasted the good word of God, and the powers of the world to come, if they shall fall away, to renew them again unto repentance; seeing they crucify to themselves the Son of God afresh, and put him to an open shame.

"Isn't that a contradiction?" the man asked. "I thought you believed it was impossible for people to fall away from grace."

"I certainly do," I said, "but that doesn't change the truthfulness of these passages. The words we have just read are true, but they are no more true than the Bible passages that we find on the other side of this issue. Jesus said, 'My Father, which gave them me, is greater than all; and no man is able to pluck them out of my Father's hand' (John 10:29).

"Then Paul said in Philippians 1:6: 'Being confident of this very thing, that he which hath begun a good work in you [the work of salvation] will perform it until the day of Jesus Christ.' Or Paul's great statement of the believer's security in Romans 8:35–39: 'Who shall separate us from the love of Christ?' Paul listed a number of things that try to separate us but cannot: tribulation, distress, persecution, famine, nakedness, peril, sword, death, life, angels, principalities, powers, height, depth, things present, things to come. And just in case he left anything out, Paul added, 'nor any other creature, shall be able to separate us from the love of God, which is in Christ Jesus our Lord.'"

The young man looked at me with an expression of helpless confusion. "But . . . but that's a contradiction, isn't it?"

TWO VIEWS

Perhaps you're thinking, *We have one list of Bible passages that say one thing, and another list that says the opposite. How do we resolve this Bible mystery?*

You are not the first to raise this question. This has been an issue within Christendom for centuries. Because of the seeming contradiction between these two lists of Bible texts, there are two camps within the Christian community. One believes in the perseverance of the saints, while the other believes that salvation is something that can be gained, then lost. Though there are many doctrines that all Christians hold in common—the deity of Christ, the Trinity, the Resurrection, and so forth—there are some things that Christians disagree about in good conscience, and this is one such issue. There are sincere, godly people on each side of this issue.

The first step toward resolving this seeming conflict is to recognize the unity of Scripture. All of Scripture is God's Word, and God speaks with one voice, not two. So we don't really have two sets of Bible texts, each saying the opposite thing. Properly understood, these passages speak in harmony. This Bible mystery has a solution, and to understand the solution, we must recognize that there is a very important difference between these two sets of biblical texts.

The Scripture passages that declare the eternal security of the believer are all *categorical, unconditional declarations of fact.* They state that nothing can separate us from God, no one can take us out of the Father's hand, and so forth. The other passages—the warnings in Hebrews and 2 Peter against falling away from the truth—are all *conditional* statements. As you read through those warnings, you see that the word *if* occurs in each one (emphasis added): "*If* . . . they are again entangled therein, and overcome," wrote Peter. And the writer to the Hebrews also stated, "*If* they shall fall away," and "*If* we sin willfully."

Christians are divided over this issue because they fail to see the difference between these two sets of passages. Those who believe it is possible to fall from grace often believe we can fall away and return, again and again.

But those who hold this position have a problem: If Christians actually do fall away and lose their salvation, these Bible texts offer no hope that such a person could ever return. In fact, those texts state that "it is *impossible* . . . to renew them again to repentance."

I don't believe the Bible teaches that a genuine Christian can lose his salvation. When Peter and the writer of Hebrews made those warning statements, they were conditional statements—if, if, if. Now, why would God put such statements in His Word if people did not actually have the capacity to fall away and lose their salvation? I can best answer this question with an example from my own experience.

When our daughter, Jennifer, was about four or five, we decided to let her play in the front yard. Until then she had only played in the fenced-in backyard, which was nice and cozy and protective. But the front yard? That was the real world!

As we opened the door to let her out in the front yard for the first time, I said, "Remember, Jennifer, you must not go out into the street, because if you go out into the street, you could get hit by a car." She promised she would stay out of the street.

But you know how little children are. She went out into the front yard and thought, *Wow! Look at this big, wide world out here! And there's the street. I'm not supposed to go there—but I actually could if I wanted to!*

What Jennifer didn't know was that her daddy was in the living room, peeking out around the edge of the drapes, watching. All she had to do was take three little steps toward the street, and I would have been right there, snatching her up so fast she wouldn't have had time to catch her breath!

You might ask, "Well, if you were going to protect her anyway, why warn her about the street?" The answer is obvious: I didn't want my daughter growing up and becoming an irresponsible adult. I wanted her to learn about the dangers of life at an early age, so that she could become wise and avoid them.

Imagine if I had never warned her of the dangers of the street. She would have gone outside, and every time she wandered near the street, her daddy would have had to run out, swoop her up, and set her down close to the house. She would have thought, *I wonder why he did that?* But because I warned her, she came to understand the dangers so that I didn't have to hover over her to keep her safe. She learned to avoid the dangers on her own.

If I, as a human father, have the sense to raise my child to recognize life's pitfalls and snares, how much wiser must our Father in heaven be? As Charles Hodge has put it, God wants to "rear us up" by moral, not magical, means. He wants us to grow to understand and respect His moral law. He does not want to have to swoop down and rescue us by miraculous, magical means because we haven't learned to recognize life's dangers. So He gives us these warnings in His Word.

At the same time, we also have this wonderful promise of the perseverance of the saints. We can know beyond all doubt that we will be kept and enabled to persevere, since only those who persevere to the end shall be saved. But we also must listen to the warnings. Those warnings are there for us, not for others, lest we deceive ourselves and find at last that we have never been saved at all.

Dear friend, are you a saint? If so, you are persevering unto the end, and God will never let you go.

PERSEVERING GRACE

The sincere but mistaken doctrine that a genuine Christian can lose his or her salvation has produced untold fear and grief in Christians through the centuries. Those who rely on their own perseverance rather than the persevering grace of God for their salvation live in a continual state of spiritual and emotional torment. *What if I sin and die before I can repent and be saved once more?*

We see this tragic lack of assurance in the life of Emperor Constantine the Great. Constantine was the son of a pagan ruler, Constantius Chlorus, and Helena, a Christian believer. Though influenced by his Christian mother, young Constantine was raised by his father to follow the old Roman gods. But when young Constantine compared the savagery of the Romans with the love and courage of the Christians, he became conflicted inside. He felt God tugging at his heart—yet he could not let go of the pagan ways.

In A.D. 312, as he prepared to go to war against an insurgent, Constantine had a vision. He saw a shining cross in the sky bearing the inscription, "In this sign, conquer." Then the Lord Jesus appeared to him in a dream, telling him that with the sign of the cross he would defeat the enemy. The next day, Constantine ordered that the symbol of the cross be emblazoned on all the pennants and shields of his army. That day, his army was victorious.

Soon after the victory, Constantine made a personal profession of faith in Jesus Christ. In a short time, Christianity went from being an outlawed religion to being a state religion, changing not only the course of Christian history, but also the history of the world. Constantine moved the capital of the empire from Rome to a new capital, Constantinople, and ordered the construction of many Christian churches in place of the old pagan temples. He also convened the first great Church council at Nicaea in A.D. 325.

Strangely, however, Constantine refused to be baptized until the spring of A.D. 337, as he felt death approaching. Why? Because he did not know for sure that he could persevere in his faith. He did not trust his own faithfulness. Only in his last days, as he lay at death's doorstep, did he finally gain the confidence to believe that he would not lose his salvation. That, indeed, is very sad. God never intended for Christians to live under such a cloud of uncertainty.

If it is your heart's desire to follow Christ, He will give you the grace to persevere until that day when you stand before Him, faultless at the judgment bar. The entire universe will be astonished to see that we—mere flesh-and-blood Christians—were able to persevere through life. That accomplishment will not be the result of any power or determination of our own. No, what will amaze the world is the incredible mercy and power of God.

So persevere, my friend! Heed the warnings, and take hold of the promises—for *both* are equally true.

Mystery 2

IS IT POSSIBLE
NOT TO SIN?

"I t is my belief, Watson," Sherlock Holmes once said, "founded upon my experience, that the lowest and vilest alleys in London do not present a more dreadful record of sin than does the smiling and beautiful countryside." To which his friend Dr. Watson, replied, "You horrify me!"

There is much wisdom in that fragment of dialogue from Sir Arthur Conan Doyle's story "The Adventure of the Copper Beeches." Holmes knew all too well that sin knows no boundaries. It not only pervades the alleys and slums, but it also pervades the sunny countryside, the opulent penthouses, and the affluent suburbs. If we are honest with ourselves, we must admit that sin even roosts among our church pews on Sunday mornings. No wonder Dr. Watson was horrified! We should all be horrified by the presence of sin in our lives!

But are we horrified by sin? Or are we complacent and casual about it—both our own sin and the sin of those around us? If we truly understood God's view of sin, as He has expressed it in His Word, we would not be so casual about sin as we seem to be.

What does God say about sin in His Word? Ah, my friend, therein lies our next Bible mystery!

CAN CHRISTIANS LIVE A SINLESS LIFE?

There is a New Testament passage that troubles many Christians: "Whosoever is born of God doth not commit sin; for his seed remaineth in him: and he cannot sin" (1 John 3:9). You and I both know that it is impossible, even as committed Christians, to live a sinless life. So why does this verse tell us that we must live completely without sin?

The true meaning of 1 John 3:9 is accessible only if you know something about Greek, the language in which the New Testament was originally written. In Greek, verbs generally have less to do with time and more to do with the nature of the action. The Greek present tense is called the *linear tense,* and this tense involves an action that is repeated over and over, like waves continuously breaking on the shore. One of the Greek past tenses is called the *aorist tense,* and it involves an event that happened at a single point in time.

The Greek verbs in 1 John 3:9 are in the present linear tense, the tense that speaks of a continual or repeated action. So a translation of this verse that would accurately capture the sense of the original Greek would be, "Whosoever is born of God does not *continue in the practice of sin,* for his seed *continues to remain* in him, and he cannot *continue in the habit of sin* because he is born of God."

The great Protestant theologians and Greek New Testament scholars agree with this rendering of 1 John 3:9:

- Dr. A. T. Robinson, one of the leading American scholars of ancient Greek: "The present active infinitive . . . can only mean 'and he cannot go on sinning.'"

- Matthew Henry, the eminent Bible commentator: "He cannot continue in the course and practice of sin."

- John Calvin, the great Reformer: "What the Apostle contends for stands unalterable, that the design of regeneration is to destroy sin, and that all who are born of God lead a righteous and a holy life, because the Spirit of God restrains the lusting of sin."

So the meaning is clear in the original Greek passage: Genuinely born-again children of God do commit occasional sins, because there are remnants of the old sin nature in all of us. But the seed of God remains in us so that our hearts desire holy things, and the old nature and its lusts, though present, do not rule over us. Paul put it this way: "Sin shall not have dominion over you" (Rom. 6:14).

It's one thing to have occasional sin in your life. It's another thing for sin to have dominion over you. Sin does not rule over the life of a genuine Christian. Those who are born of God cannot continue in the habit and practice of sin, because the seed of God lives in them. What is this seed of God? John uses the Greek word *sperma*, as in the sperm seed that creates life. In other words, the seed of God creates a new life, a new and distinctive nature within the Christian—a nature that does not desire sin, but desires God's righteousness and holiness.

When a person comes into a saving relationship with Christ, the Lord implants a new nature within that person—one that abhors sin. When you come to Christ, you receive Him not only as Savior, but also as Lord. You can call someone "Lord" only if you serve and obey Him.

Does that mean that a genuine Christian never sins? No. A genuine Christian will occasionally fall into sin—but he will not live in that sin in an ongoing way. A genuine Christian will not pursue sin, bask in sin, or luxuriate in it. A genuine Christian, even though experiencing temptation as a normal part of life, will nevertheless look upon sin as a horror and a betrayal of the One who was nailed to the cross by sin.

Some folks call themselves Christians, but they wallow in sin like a pig wallows in the mud. "Ah, look at that wonderful mud puddle," they say to themselves, pondering their sin.

Yet there are others, genuine Christians, who are more like sheep than pigs. A sheep may, on occasion, fall into a mud puddle. But sheep do not wallow in mud. If they fall in, they get up as fast as they can and are not satisfied until they have cleaned all the mud off their fleecy white wool.

So there is a major difference between the genuine believer and a person who professes belief yet lives like an unbeliever. These two kinds of people are as different as a pig is from a sheep.

I once officiated at the funeral of a man who died in his mid-forties. Before the service, I talked with his mother, and she shared with me that her late son had lived a terribly ungodly life. He had been a drunkard and a womanizer, a drug user, and a criminal. "But it's a blessing to know that my Johnny went to Heaven," she concluded. I wondered how she knew that! "Well," she explained, "when he was twelve, Johnny accepted Jesus as his Savior. I know he never went to church after that, and he lived a terribly sinful life, but at least he made that decision when he was twelve."

Now, I wasn't about to tell a grieving mother the real truth about her son's eternal fate. But I can tell you this: I would *not* want to go into eternity handcuffed to Johnny! The Bible never teaches that faith in Christ is just a meaningless one-time profession, a "fire insurance policy" against an eternity in Hell and nothing more.

God wants to root sin out of your life—not because He wants to kill your fun, but because He wants you to have *joy*. The world tells you that there is pleasure in sinning, but God tells you the truth: Sin brings nothing but misery. Joy can be found only in obedience to Him. When you are engaged in sin, you are far from His joy. The joy that awaits us in Heaven is the joy of having every stain of sin removed, the joy of being made eternally pure.

THE CHASTENING LOVE OF GOD

God loves us as His children. All good and loving parents discipline their children, and God, our loving heavenly Father, is no exception.

In fact, He is the ultimate example of a loving parent. The book of Hebrews tells us, "For whom the Lord loveth he chasteneth, and scourgeth every son whom he receiveth. If ye endure chastening, God dealeth with you as with sons; for what son is he whom the father chasteneth not?" (Heb. 12:6–7) The writer went on to say that no chastening is joyous in the present time. It is grievous and painful—but it yields a pleasant and peaceable "fruit of righteousness" in our lives (v. 11).

If you are living a lifestyle of sin and *not* experiencing the chastening hand of God, you should ask yourself whether you are truly a child of God. And if you are now experiencing the chastening love of your heavenly Father, then I urge you to respond to that love, receive the benefit of that chastening, and renew your commitment to serve Him as your Lord and Savior.

God chastens His children in twelve distinct ways. If you, as a genuine Christian, commit a willful sin, you can expect to experience one or more of these forms of God's loving discipline in your life:

1. Loss of joy. When we turn our backs on Christ, we lose the joy of our salvation. Remember the cry of David: "Restore unto me the joy of thy salvation . . . and sinners shall be converted unto thee" (Ps. 51:12–13). Are you experiencing the joy of your salvation—or has sin bled the joy out of your life?

2. Loss of the assurance of salvation. A Christian who is living obediently before God is able to sing with conviction, "Blessed assurance, Jesus is mine! / O, what a foretaste of glory divine!"[1] Sin diminishes that assurance and causes us to doubt our salvation. That is a form of God's chastening designed to draw us back into His loving arms.

3. Loss of the peace of God. His peace comes as a direct result of the assurance of our salvation. When we lack that assurance because of sin in our lives, we lose our peace with God. Our soul is in turmoil. Again, this is not a matter of God wanting to hurt us. It is a Father's chastening love, urging us to return to Him.

4. Loss of fruitfulness for God. Jesus taught that only branches that have been cleansed and purged will bear good fruit. Perhaps you were once very fruitful in the Christian life, but no longer are. You wonder what has happened to diminish your fruitfulness. You try to witness to people, but they will not receive what you say. It could be that sin inhibits your fruitfulness for God. The solution is to humbly respond to God's chastening and return to Him in obedience and repentance.

5. *Loss of interest in spiritual things.* The Bible refers to this condition as "hardening of the heart." Has your heart become hardened? Have you lost interest in spiritual things? Remember when your faith was new and exciting and alive? There was once a time when you showed up every time the church doors were open. Your love of prayer and Bible study knew no bounds. Your witness for Christ was vibrant and bold. Now, however, you rarely talk to God, rarely open His Word, hardly talk to others about Christ, and it has become a terrible chore to drag your bones to one Sunday service a week! Why? Because your heart has become hardened due to sin in your life. Don't let that condition prevail in your life for another day. Yield to the chastening love of your Father in heaven.

6. *Loss of a sense of God's guidance.* The Scripture says: "In all thy ways acknowledge him, and he shall direct thy paths" (Prov. 3:6). When you are involved in sin, you don't want to acknowledge God. You don't want to even think about Him. Consequently, the Holy Spirit cannot guide your life. So you are adrift, and you quickly lose your way. You experience confusion, indecision, and bafflement. You become lost. You fall into traps and snares. But you don't have to remain in that condition. Acknowledge God and obey Him. Respond to His chastening love—and He will direct your paths once more.

7. *Loss of health.* Let's be very clear on this point: When a person is sick, it does not mean that he has sinned. Job's so-called comforters tried to convince him that his illness and affliction were the result of sin in his life, but God ultimately rebuked them for their error. Jesus also rebuked His disciples for the same error when they asked Him, "Who did sin, this man, or his parents, that he was born blind?" His

reply: "Neither hath this man sinned, nor his parents: but that the works of God should be made manifest in him" (John 9:2–3). Illness and injury are a normal part of life.

But we also know that there is a connection between a clear conscience and a healthy body. Sin can often make us sick, as even doctors will tell you. The Bible tells us not to worry, but to trust God; when we ignore that sound advice from God, we become prey to ulcers, high blood pressure, headaches, and other physical problems. Guilt, too, can produce physical symptoms, from sleeplessness to digestive disorders. Though there is no way we can guarantee good health at all times, we can eliminate one source of illness if we turn to Christ and surrender to His Lordship.

8. Loss of prosperity. We see this principle at work in the life of Israel in the Old Testament. The Israelites had sinned against God. They had not brought their tithes and offerings in obedience to His commands. They thought that they could ignore His law and still be able to gather much wealth. But God said, "Ye have sown much, and bring in little . . . and he that earneth wages earneth wages to put it into a bag with holes . . . Ye looked for much, and, lo, it came to little; and when ye brought it home, I did blow upon it" (Hag. 1:6, 9).

God has put in place systems designed to destroy the wealth of those who turn their backs upon Him. Why? Because God hates His people? No! Because He loves them and wants them to worship Him, not money.

9. Family losses. Sometimes, when people fall into grievous sins and will not return, God must use a heavier and more grievous rod of chastening. He did this with King David when he committed the heinous, destructive sins of adultery with Bathsheba and the murder of Bathsheba's husband. Three of David's children died because of that sin. Does that mean that when a parent loses a child, it is proof of some sin in that parent's life? Of course not. Tragedy comes into our lives for many reasons, and those reasons may not have anything to do with sin. But we should examine ourselves and make sure we are not engaging in any grievous sin that might invite the hand of God's most severe discipline in our lives.

10. Loss to the Church. The sin of Christians can cause loss to a church. If you want to see what Jesus thinks of the Church, read the first few chapters of Revelation. There He warns that the sin of certain members of the church will cause the light or "lampstand" of that church to be removed. I have been to many of the historic sites in Asia Minor (modern-day Turkey) that are mentioned in that opening section of Revelation. I can tell you that in most cases those churches are no longer there. God did indeed remove those lampstands. Friend in Christ, is there a sin in your life that is hurting the Church and its progress in the world?

11. Loss to the kingdom. The sin of God's people can cause loss to a whole kingdom—to the kingdom of Israel, and even to the kingdom of God. We see this principle at work in Joshua 7, where Achan sinned at Ai. This man of Israel had stolen bars of gold and silver, along with garments and other goods, which had been condemned by God, and he had hidden them in his tent. He thought no one would ever discover his secret sin. But when the soldiers of Israel went out to conquer the city, they were overwhelmed by a much smaller force. Israel had been undermined by Achan's sin, and hundreds died as a result.

Do not assume that no one else is affected by your sin. Make no mistake: The entire kingdom of God is affected by the sin of a single person. Don't allow sin to gain a foothold in your life.

12. Loss of life. Your sin—the sin of a child of God—can literally bring about your premature death in this world. Consider what the Bible says about those who sinned concerning the Lord's Supper. They were taking those symbols of tremendous sacrifice with unclean and impenitent hands, not repenting of their sins. God, speaking through Paul, said, "For this cause many are weak and sickly among you and many sleep [have died]" (1 Cor. 11:30).

I recall a man I knew in our church—a fairly young man who had once been a minister. Outwardly, he seemed to be a godly man, but he had committed the sin of adultery with a married woman. Instead of repenting, he urged this woman to divorce her husband and marry him. I admonished the man and implored him to repent, but he refused. He was brought before the discipline committee of the church, who also admonished him; again he refused. He was suspended from the sacraments of the church, but still he did not repent. Finally, the ruling elders of our church concluded that it was necessary to excommunicate this man. But before it could happen, the young man suddenly died.

I do not believe this man's death at such a young age was a coincidence. I believe it was the loving yet chastening hand of God, dealing with a man who resisted every appeal to repent and submit himself to the Lordship of Christ. Sometimes, when sin is severe, the discipline of God is proportionately severe.

These are just some of the ways God may choose to chasten those He loves, those who are truly His own and yet continue in impenitent sin. My friends, we need to take the warnings of God seriously, because they are very real. But, thank God, we can also take the promises seriously, for they are just as real.

WHICH IS TRUE—
PREDESTINATION OR
FREE WILL?

Isaac Bashevis Singer, the Jewish-American short story writer (winner of the Nobel Prize for Literature, 1978), was once asked whether he believed in predestination or in free will. "We have to believe in free will," he replied wryly. "We have *no choice.*"

The Bible tells us that we must choose life and choose Christ—yet it also tells us that God predestines us to salvation! This seems contradictory, doesn't it? For surely if we have free will in the matter of our salvation, then there can be no predestination. And if we are predestined to salvation, then we seem to have no choice, no free will, in the matter.

Many Christians seem surprised to learn that the doctrine of predestination—that God in His sovereignty chose us from the beginning, before the foundation of the world, to be saved—is even in the Bible. I find this strange, since predestination is mentioned in the Bible so frequently. A prime example is 2 Thessalonians 2:13 (emphasis added).

But we are bound to give thanks alway to God for you, brethren beloved of the Lord, *because God hath from the beginning chosen you to salvation* through sanctification of the Spirit and belief of the truth.

23

In this chapter we will look at several more biblical statements about predestination, and we will solve such mysteries as: What is predestination? If we are predestined to salvation, do we truly have free will?

THE FORGOTTEN DOCTRINE

The doctrine of predestination has fallen on hard times in recent years. To some, it is a strange doctrine—it seems almost foreign to Christianity. Most Christians, I daresay, have never even heard one sermon on predestination. Yet it is a fact that the doctrine of predestination is one of the essential doctrines of orthodox Protestantism.

The list of those who have firmly upheld the doctrine of predestination reads like a Who's Who of the Protestant Reformation. Martin Luther was a tremendous predestinarian. In fact, all of the Protestant reformers, including John Calvin, John Knox, Theodore Beza, and Ulrich Zwingli, were strong predestinarians. One historian called the doctrine of predestination "the Hercules might of the young Reformation." It was this doctrine that took salvation out of the hands of men (thus out of the hands of the Pope), and put it in the hands of the sovereign God.

Not only was predestination the authoritative view throughout all Protestant nations and denominations, but it was not until 260 years after the Reformation that there was even one denomination that denied the doctrine of predestination. In fact, it has been suggested that whatever morality may be found today in the nations where the Reformation began—in Germany, England, Scotland, Switzerland, or Holland—is due to the lingering effects of the doctrine of efficacious grace and absolute predestination.

I hope you are beginning to sense how far the Protestant Church has fallen away from its Reformation heritage—so far that what was once a foundational principle has become a strange and foreign doctrine. Why has this happened? I am convinced that the reason is the pride of humanity—the refusal of human will to submit to any other will, including the will of God. There is no doubt in my mind that the widespread ignorance and rejection of this central doctrine of Scripture by the modern Church is influenced by the intrusive rise of humanism, which has elevated man to the place of God and (in its vain human imagination) has ejected God from His throne.

Over the centuries the doctrine of predestination has had its ups and downs within the Church. If you chart the level of acceptance of this doctrine alongside a chart of the vitality and impact of the Church on society, you will see an amazing correlation. Whenever the Church has been morally effective and triumphant in the world, it has been when the Church has actively proclaimed the doctrines of the Almighty's grace, sovereignty, and predestinating love. Conversely, whenever morality has declined and humanism has ascended and the Church has slipped into a state of lukewarm apathy or outright depravity, the doctrine of predestination has been lost. Decline and corruption are the inevitable fruit of the denial of the sovereign and electing grace of Almighty God.

IS PREDESTINATION BIBLICAL?

Is predestination taught by Scripture? If this doctrine is not biblical, then it doesn't matter what its tradition is or who may have espoused it in the last five hundred years. If it is not biblical, it is not true.

When we turn to the Bible, the arbiter of all truth, we find numerous emphatic statements about God's sovereign and gracious predestination, His foreordination, His election of believers, or the calling of His Spirit upon our lives. Here are just a few examples (with references to predestination italicized):

In Matthew 24:31, Jesus said, "And he [the Son of man] shall send his angels with a great sound of a trumpet, and they shall gather together *his elect* from the four winds, from one end of heaven to the other." In Mark 13:20, Jesus made another prediction of the last days: "And except that the Lord had shortened those days, no flesh should be saved: but *for the elect's sake, whom he hath chosen*, he hath shortened the days." In verse 22, He predicted the rise of false Christs and false prophets who will work amazing pseudo-miracles and wonders in an effort "to seduce, if it were possible, even *the elect*." And in Luke 18:7–8, Jesus said of those who suffer for His sake: "And shall not God avenge *his own elect* . . . I tell you that he will avenge them speedily." Predestination—God's sovereign calling and election in our lives—was a key concept in the teaching of Jesus.

Predestination also pervades the writings of Paul. One of the most beloved passages in Scripture is Romans 8:28: "And we know that all things work together for good to them that love God, *to them who are the called according to his purpose*." In the next two verses, Paul hammered home the doctrine of predestination: "For whom he did *foreknow*, he also did *predestinate* to be conformed to the image of his Son, that he might be the firstborn among many brethren. Moreover whom he did *predestinate*, them he also *called*: and whom he *called*, them he also justified: and whom he justified, them he also glorified" (vv. 29–30). In verse 33, he added, "Who shall lay any thing to the charge of God's *elect*? It is God that justifieth."

Many people quote Romans 8:28 out of context, saying, "All things work together for good." That statement is heresy and a lie. All things do not simply work together for good. All things work together for good *only* to *God's elect*. The world is filled with people who live miserable, wretched, sinful lives. They are born in their sins and they die in their sins. They come to judgment. They are condemned and suffer eternal punishment. Everything does not work together for good in their lives. But for God's own chosen children, everything—even painful and tragic circumstances—can be woven into His plan to bring forth good.

God has predestined us to be conformed to the image of His Son. He chose us before the foundation of the world. All of those He has called will come unto Him and be justified.

In Ephesians 1:5, Paul wrote, "Having *predestinated* us unto the adoption of children by Jesus Christ to himself, *according to the good pleasure of his will*." Can the doctrine of predestination be stated any more plainly than that? In verse 11, Paul added, "In whom also we have obtained an inheritance, being *predestinated* according to the purpose of him who worketh all things after the counsel of his own will." In Colossians 3:12, Paul described the character qualities of "the *elect* of God," qualities of "mercies, kindness, humbleness of mind, meekness, longsuffering," and so forth. Is the doctrine of predestination important? Without question.

Peter, too, addressed the doctrine of predestination in both of his letters, referring to those who would read and receive his letters as "*elect* according to the *foreknowledge* of God the Father" (1 Peter 1:2), while urging them (2 Peter 1:10), "Wherefore the rather, brethren, give diligence to *make your calling and election sure*: for if ye do these things, ye shall never fall."

Do you know that you are elect of God, chosen of God, predestined to adoption as a child of God before the beginning of time? You can know that for certain.

WHY SOME AND NOT OTHERS?

Now, the question that obviously occurs is this: Why has God predestined some people and not others? If you are one of God's chosen and elect, why has He chosen you?

We catch a glimpse of the answer in Matthew 11. There we see Jesus after He has preached to Bethsaida and Chorazin and other cities. His message has been rejected. He has been rejected. The hearts of the people in those cities are like stone. So what does Jesus do? Does He sit by the roadside and wring his hands, moaning about how He has failed? No. He turns to God the Father and says, "I thank thee, O Father, Lord of heaven and earth, because thou hast hid these things from the wise and prudent, and hast revealed them unto babes. Even so, Father: *for so it seemed good in thy sight*" (Matt. 11:25–26, emphasis added).

That, my friend, is the answer—the only answer you will ever receive. Why has God chosen you? *For so it seemed good in God's sight* to choose you. We have been predestined according to the good and perfect will of God. He works all things together after the counsel of His own good will.

God is sovereign. Whatever God does, He does because it seems good in His sight. That is the answer—the only answer we need, the only answer there will ever be.

One thing God tells us quite emphatically: He does not choose anyone because of that person's abilities, brilliance, or greatness. Being predestined by God is not a source of pride to anyone. As Paul told us in 1 Corinthians 1:26–27, "For ye see your calling, brethren, how that not many wise men after the flesh, not many mighty, not many noble, are called: But God hath chosen the foolish things of the world to confound the wise; and God hath chosen the weak things of the world to confound the things which are mighty."

How's that for an ego deflater? If God has chosen and called you, it is not because you are wise or mighty or noble, but because you are foolish and weak. That is the kind of person God calls and chooses to use to accomplish His eternal plan! So if you have been predestined by God, you have nothing whatever to boast about. The call of God upon your life and mine is a call to utter humility.

That is why Paul went on to say, "But he that glorieth, let him glory in the Lord" (2 Cor. 10:17). You and I are base and foolish and foul and weak—but the great and gracious almighty God has elected to save us. We have nothing to boast of but *Jesus Himself.*

WHAT ABOUT THE LOST?

Now, if some are the elect, then it stands to reason that other people are the non-elect. That's the aspect we find disturbing. It bothers us that some are predestined for salvation and some are not. It seems arbitrary and unfair.

And yet, if we examine the Scriptures carefully, we find a subtle but very explicit truth: The Bible never says that anyone is predestined to Hell. Again and again we see that people are predestined (elected) to salvation—but nowhere do we see that anyone is ever predestined to condemnation or Hell.

When we think of God as unfairly, arbitrarily electing people to Heaven or Hell, it is as if we have a mental picture of a row of people sitting on a fence, and God passes down the line and points at each one, "It's Hell for you, Heaven for you, Hell, Hell, Hell, Heaven, Hell . . . " Now, that *would* be unfair—and absolutely capricious! But that's not the kind of God we love and serve.

God has graciously created human beings with a free will. Using that awesome God-given power, we have chosen to plunge our race into sin. We are totally incapacitated by sin. Though we have the freedom to do whatever we *want*, we do not have the freedom to do what we *ought*, because sin is at work within us. That is why Jesus said, "If the Son therefore shall make you free, ye shall be free indeed" (John 8:36). Until He sets us free to do what we *ought* instead of merely what we *want*, we are never truly free. The idea that a person apart from God is free to do as he or she ought is a delusion.

One of Martin Luther's great theological works was *The Bondage of the Will*—a volume that contended against the views of both the Roman Catholics and the Renaissance humanists. Luther's view was that the will of human beings is like a "dumb ass ridden by the devil." I can't think of a more accurate and insightful metaphor to describe our human will.

In this humanistic age, in which we keep hearing about our "right to choose," we have to ask, Where is this vaunted "freedom of the will"? The more people indulge in their so-called freedoms, the deeper they sink into bondage. People are free to drink themselves into a stupor— and the result is an addiction to alcohol that few ever escape. People are free to use drugs, to engage in promiscuous sex, to gamble away the mortgage money—and so our social landscape is littered with the wreckage of human lives bound up in drug addiction, sex addiction, and gambling addiction. People are free to pursue power, money, and fame. And when they achieve it, they discover that their ambitions hold their lives in an unbreakable grip; they have gained the world, but lost their souls. People are told they should express their anger freely; the spiritual fruit of gentleness and self-control has fallen into disrepute— and the result is that many are now trapped and controlled by their emotions, and they have become helpless "rageaholics." We are so free that it is amazing! We are in shackles and bondage.

Again, if the Son makes you free, you shall be free indeed. Shackles are broken and slaves set free at Calvary.

So God makes His sovereign selection from among the human race, a race of sinful and corrupt people, all of whom deserve condemnation. But God extends mercy to a vast multitude. He must be just, but He doesn't have to extend mercy to any. Those whom He selects are saved—a great number out of every tribe and tongue and nation. He sends His Spirit to them to draw them to Himself.

But what about the rest? Note carefully: God invites them all to come. With a sincere invitation, He offers them a free salvation, paid for at the cost of His own dear Son. If anyone in the world will come to Jesus Christ, that person will receive the free gift of eternal life. "All that the Father giveth me," says Jesus, "shall come to me; and him that cometh to me I will in no wise cast out" (John 6:37). The problem is that no one will come! As Paul told us in 1 Corinthians 2:14, "But the natural man receiveth not the things of the Spirit of God: for they are foolishness unto him: neither can he know them, because they are spiritually discerned."

Now, God is not obligated to show mercy to anyone who has rebelled against His law, who has trampled upon the sacrifice of His Son and wreaked havoc in God's universe through a life of sin. God does not *owe* mercy to anyone. As Charles Haddon Spurgeon observed, "The amazing thing is not that everybody isn't saved, but that *anybody* is saved." It was also Spurgeon who insightfully asked, "What good is a 'whosoever will' in a world where everybody won't?"

Those whom God calls are made willing, and those who are willing, come. But what about those who are not willing? They will not come. God does not cast anyone out. He does not bar the door. Those who are outside are outside by their own choice, because they keep God away. It is not God who says, "You shall be lost," but the willfully unwilling who tell God, "Get lost! I've got plans for my life, and they don't include You."

Predestination is simply God saying, "I will have mercy on whom I will have mercy." So, in a world where all have sinned, where all fall short, where no one is righteous, how can God be criticized for extending mercy to a sinner? How can God be criticized for providing the gift of eternal life to people who are lost in their sins? And what difference does it make *when* He made this decision? Is it wrong if God made the decision yesterday to extend mercy today? Is it wrong if He made the decision last week or last year or ten years ago? Then why would it be wrong if He made that decision before the beginning of time?

For that is what predestination is—a decision that our sovereign, gracious, loving Almighty God made from all eternity when He looked ahead to a world of lost and rebellious sinners. It's a decision He made to save a vast multitude of them through His Son, Jesus. Predestination excludes no one. It keeps no one out of Heaven; it sends no one to Hell.

But it does keep many *out* of Hell. If not for God's sovereign predestination, Heaven would be empty, and Hell would be full!

Because you are reading this book, odds are that you are a follower of Christ who wants to grow deeper in the Christian faith. In that case, you are one of God's elect, chosen before the foundation of the world. I urge you, then, to be even more diligent to make your calling and election sure, for if you do these things, you will never stumble.

And if you have never given your life to Christ before, do so right now! If you seek Him, He will never turn you out. By choosing Him today, you can know for sure that He has first chosen you!

SHOULD WE JUDGE
OR NOT JUDGE?

I n the fall of 1999, the *Dallas Morning News* published a column by Shavahn Dorris, who was then a junior at Texas Christian University. In that column, entitled "Don't Be a Closet Christian," Miss Dorris confessed:

> I am a closet Christian.
>
> As closet Christians, we pray in secret. We read our Bible when we are alone. And we stray away from conversations on premarital sex, homosexuality or evolution out of fear that we might expose ourselves . . .
>
> What is the real reason we are afraid to disclose our secret? Well, maybe it is because many people will think that if you are a Christian, you are boring, intolerant and judgmental. If someone loves the Chicago Bulls and wears a Michael Jordan T-shirt, he is considered a fan, but if he loves God and wears an "I love Jesus" T-shirt, he is considered a fanatic . . .
>
> Those distorted views of Christianity lead many people to shun Christians or label them as crazy. But the fact is, shunning people because of what or how they believe is intolerant. And blindly assigning labels to people because they are proud of what they value is judgmental.

Other people's intolerance, however, isn't a good excuse for hiding one's faith. Faith is supposed to be unshakable, immovable and shameless. If not, it simply is a worthless and expendable belief.[1]

This college student speaks for many Christians. We have allowed ourselves to be driven into the closet, silenced by the fear of being labeled judgmental and intolerant because of our Christian beliefs. We have tried to make peace with a degenerate society. We have tried to placate and befriend an immoral and lawless society. We have silenced our witness. We have compromised our truth. And as we have retreated to our closets of silence, the world has become even more immoral and lawless.

All around us we see that every commandment is broken, every sinful and indecent act is applauded, every immoral lifestyle is celebrated. Today we live in a licentious and evil society in which there is only one remaining virtue: tolerance. Tolerance is the last virtue of a totally degenerate society.

When there is only one virtue left, there remains only one sin—the "sin" of intolerance, the act of being judgmental, of judging the behavior and lifestyle of other people. Although it is almost exclusively Christians who are accused of this "sin," those who would condemn Christians for their intolerance delight in calling the Bible to the witness stand to testify against Christians for their supposed intolerance. There is one statement from Scripture that every corrupt politician, every adulterer and fornicator, every prostitute and pornographer, every sinner of every stripe seems to know by heart: "Judge not!"

Tune in to any television talk show, and you will find that virtually nothing is unacceptable today: adultery, fornication, homosexuality, lying, stealing, cheating, mate-swapping, incest, and unspeakable perversions. All behavior is perfectly acceptable except that one heinous, vile, contemptible "sin"—judging someone else's sin. When an American president is caught in the Oval Office doing in a public place what should not even be whispered in private, a chorus of defenders cries out, "Judge not!" When pedophiles openly demand the right to exploit your children for their own gratification, they demand, "Judge not!" When gay rights activists parade indecently in the streets, when criminals loot and rob and kill, when rock stars and movie stars behave obscenely onscreen and off, their critics are silenced with shouts of "Judge not!"

It was Jesus who first spoke those words. "Judge not," He said, "that ye be not judged. For with what judgment ye judge, ye shall be judged: and with what measure ye mete, it shall be measured to you again" (Matt. 7:1–2). People who couldn't recite another verse of Scripture are quick to recite those two words, "Judge not!" They cling to those words with religious fervor and spout them with evangelical zeal. "What right have you to judge my behavior?" they say. "Jesus said, 'Judge not!'"

Yet those of us who have more than a nodding acquaintance with God's Word are well aware that while some passages in the Bible tell us to judge not, other passages tell us to judge! So what is the truth of the matter? Are we to judge or not to judge?

WHAT DOES THE BIBLE SAY?

During the presidential scandal of 1998, many journalists and columnists took upon themselves the unaccustomed mantle of Bible expositors. "Adultery," wrote one presidential defender in the media, "happens to be one of the few sins about which Jesus Christ spoke directly and unequivocally." Citing the story of Jesus' rescue of the woman caught in adultery in John 8, this columnist quoted the Lord's words, "He that is without sin among you, let him first cast a stone at her" (John 8:7). He gave the impression that Jesus' entire message to this woman was one of nonjudgmentalism and outright tolerance for sin. He quoted part of Jesus' words in verse 11—"Neither do I condemn thee"—but he left out the most important part of Jesus' message to this woman: "Go, and sin no more." Jesus pardons sinners—but not without repentance on the sinners' part and not without cost to Himself, the cost of His own dear blood upon the cross. For some reason, the "tolerance police" always leave out that part of the equation.

Another presidential defender—the minister of a church the president attended—cited Paul's famous Love Chapter, 1 Corinthians 13, as a pretext for excusing sexual misdeeds in the Oval Office and tolerating crimes of perjury and obstruction of justice. In other words, Christlike forgiveness should negate all moral censure and legal consequences of the president's behavior. This minister somehow ignored the fact that just a few chapters earlier, in 1 Corinthians 5, Paul severely reprimanded the church in Corinth because it had tolerated a sexually immoral man! Paul had even told the Corinthians, "Put away from among yourselves that wicked person" (v. 13)!

So in both of these instances—in the "sermons" of both the newspaper columnist and the president's minister—we find a flawed approach to the issue of tolerance and forgiveness. Both of these "Bible expositors" went to God's Word in search of support for an attitude of total nonjudgmentalism and indulgence of sin—and both of them missed the fact that our forgiving and pardoning God is also a God who holds us accountable and expects us to hold one another accountable for our behavior. "Judge not!" is clearly not the only thing the Bible has to say about sin. The Bible also says, "Judge!"

The truth of God's Word cannot be reduced to simpleminded sloganeering. We must examine its truth carefully and precisely to understand what God is really saying to us about this matter of judging and judging not. To be able to interpret any biblical text correctly, we must observe three rules:

1. Examine the text itself to see if you understand what it says.

2. Examine the immediate context.

3. Examine the text in the whole context of the Scripture.

Let's apply these three rules of biblical interpretation to the famous text "Judge not."

First, when we examine the text, we must recognize that the New Testament was originally written in Greek. The inability to understand Greek often places us at a disadvantage when we are attempting to solve Bible mysteries. True, in most cases, our English translations give us a very good sense of the original Greek New Testament. But there are times when we must go beyond the English translation, when we must sleuth our way through to the original Greek text, to be able to capture the precise meaning of the text.

The Greek phrase that is rendered "judge not" in Matthew 7:1–2 is *krino me*, which is in the present continuous tense. In this tense, it means: "Do not *continually* be engaged in judging." Now, that is quite different from the meaning usually assigned to this phrase: "Don't *ever* judge anyone or anything."

Next, let's examine the immediate context. Look at Matthew 7:1–5:

Judge not, that ye be not judged. For with what judgment ye judge, ye shall be judged: and with what measure ye mete, it shall be measured to you again. And why beholdest thou the mote that is in thy brother's eye, but considerest not the beam that is in thine own eye? Or how wilt thou say to thy brother, Let me pull out the mote out of thine eye; and, behold, a beam is in thine own eye? Thou hypocrite, first cast out the beam out of thine own eye; and then shalt thou see clearly to cast out the mote out of thy brother's eye.

Notice that all these verses relate to judgment. Together, they explain the meaning of verse 1. Clearly, Jesus was specifically and pointedly addressing a particular problem—the sin of hypocrisy. Jesus did not say it is wrong to exercise our faculties of good judgment and moral discernment. Instead, He said that it is hypocritical and evil to continually condemn other people when we engage in the same or

36

worse sins on an ongoing basis. Only when our own lives have been cleansed and purified are we truly qualified to hold others accountable for their actions. The context makes the meaning of the "Judge not" statement unmistakably clear.

And that's not all! We move on to verse 6, and we find an astoundingly judgmental and intolerant statement! Jesus said:

> Give not that which is holy unto the dogs, neither cast ye your pearls before swine, lest they trample them under their feet, and turn again and rend you.

Twice in that verse, we are commanded to judge. Did you miss it? Look again. Jesus referred to dogs and swine—highly judgmental metaphors! When Jesus talked about dogs, He was not talking about cute little poodles or chihuahuas that jump in your lap and lick your face. He was talking about wild, mangy, vicious curs that roam the street, feeding on garbage, and sometimes even killing children.

As far as swine are concerned, I think the meaning here is again quite obvious. Pork was an unclean food for a Jew. You will recall that the Prodigal Son, having spent all of the money he received from his father, went to work feeding swine—*swine*, of all things!

In Matthew 7 Jesus compared some people to dogs and swine. If this is not a judgmental statement, what is? He was saying that it is unwise to put what is holy and valuable and sacred in front of dogs and hogs, because they will only trample them and turn on you and destroy you. Therefore, you must exercise judgment.

Christ's words are true. Almost everyone who has ever shared the Gospel with other people has encountered the kind of person Jesus describes—the kind of person who demonstrates a doglike or swinish attitude toward God and Christ and the Bible, toward all things holy. Jesus was saying here that it is pointless and even dangerous to spend the rest of your life trying to win these dogs or swine to Christ. There are others who are eagerly seeking God, indicating that the Holy Spirit is at work in their lives, so you turn your back on the dogs and swine. Leave them to their doggishness or swinishness.

Immediately after the "judge not" statement, we are told in no uncertain terms that there are times when we *must* judge. And there is more to the Matthew 7 context that sheds light on the mystery of judging or not judging.

If you examine verses 15 through 20, you see Jesus talking about false prophets:

> Beware of false prophets, which come to you in sheep's clothing, but inwardly they are ravening wolves. Ye shall know them by their fruits. Do men gather grapes of thorns, or figs of thistles? Even so every good tree bringeth forth good fruit; but a corrupt tree bringeth forth evil fruit. A good tree cannot bring forth evil fruit, neither can a corrupt tree bring forth good fruit. Every tree that bringeth not forth good fruit is hewn down, and cast into the fire. Wherefore by their fruits ye shall know them.

We are to judge people who claim to speak for God, and we will be able to judge their validity or nonvalidity, Jesus said, because they are like trees: they bear fruit. A good tree bears good fruit; a bad tree bears bad fruit. So whenever any person comes proclaiming himself a prophet or a teacher from God, you are to be a fruit inspector. If the fruit is bad, he is a false prophet. You cannot be a fruit inspector without exercising judgment.

Finally, let's look at this verse according to the third rule of biblical interpretation: Examine the text within the whole context of the Scripture. Many places in God's Word tell us that we must, at times, hold people accountable and judge their behavior. A few of these passages are 1 Corinthians 5:12; 6:1; Galatians 1:8–9; Philippians 3:2; 1 Thessalonians 2:14–15; 1 Timothy 1:6–7; Titus 3:2, 10; 1 John 4:1; 2 John 10; and 3 John 9.

Our friends who are so quick to say "Judge not," meaning that you are never supposed to judge anyone for anything, have made a major error. They have invited others to make a judgment about *them,* and the judgment I would make about such a person is, *He doesn't know what he's talking about!*

HOW DOES JESUS MEAN WE SHOULD "JUDGE NOT"?

There are times when we *must* judge, and these are clearly indicated in Scripture. Then under what circumstances should we "Judge not"?

In context, it becomes clear that Jesus was warning us not to become the kind of people who are habitual faultfinders, always looking for bad things in other people. Such people are nothing but "bad fruit inspectors." Bad fruit is all they seek and all they find. Even if there is no bad fruit to be found in other people, they seem to find it anyway. Jesus described their tragic nature in these verses. In verses 3 through 5, Jesus employs ironic humor (no doubt drawn from his background as a carpenter) to suggest that while such people claim to be good at spotting the little dust mote in another person's eye, they can't even see the huge piece of lumber that is lodged in their own eye!

Now, that's a very funny visual image when you think about it—one man saying to another, "Here, brother, let me pull the speck out of your eye"—yet he can't even get close to the other man because this huge piece of timber is projecting out of his eye and gouging the ground in front of him! But this humorous image is not so funny when you actually have to deal with the hypocrite with the lumber in his eye. Such people can be extremely aggravating and painful to be around.

To be a habitual faultfinder is a tragic thing. To live with one can be even more tragic. The sad thing is that many habitual faultfinders can read this statement of Jesus and not even realize He is talking about them! "Oh, I just can't stand that kind of person!" the faultfinder may say. "I'm so glad I'm not that sort of person!" The Pharisees of Jesus' time were like that. They had a self-righteous, condemning spirit. They were without mercy, without love. Worst of all, their consciences were seared and their eyes were blinded by logs of pride and arrogance so that God could not reach them with the truth of their own sin.

Why are some people so fault-finding and critical of others? Dr. Martin Lloyd Jones, the former heart surgeon to the queen of England, left the medical profession and went to theological seminary, emerging as a great minister with a keen insight into the spiritual heart of humanity. He once said, "What is this spirit that condemns? It is a self-righteous spirit. Self is always at the back of it, and it is always a manifestation of self-righteousness and a sense of superiority."

Self-righteousness and pride—these are the sins Jesus warns us against in this passage. There is a big difference between self-righteous judgmentalism and godly, righteous judgment. The problem with the sins of self-righteous pride is that the faultfinder cannot see them—at least not in himself. Yet these sins are more serious than almost any sin the faultfinder discovers in the people around him. Pride, after all, is the first and worst sin. It is the sin by which Satan fell.

Even the master detective, Sherlock Holmes, understood the value of humility and the danger of self-righteous pride. In "The Boscombe Valley Mystery," there is a scene in which Holmes says to a man who has committed crimes in order to save his family:

> Well, it is not for me to judge you. I pray that [I] may never be exposed to such a temptation . . . I never heard of such a case as this that I do not think . . . "There, but for the grace of God, goes Sherlock Holmes."

THE RIGHT WAY TO JUDGE

"For with what judgment ye judge," Jesus said, "*ye shall be judged:* and with what measure ye mete, *it shall be measured to you* again" (emphasis added). These are sobering words. Jesus makes us aware that when we judge others, we will be judged by the very same standard we apply to them. Yes, we are called to judge others—but soberly, righteously, and humbly, not pridefully and self-righteously. The Bible gives clear guidance for exercising judgment and accountability toward others. The key New Testament passage in this regard is found in Galatians 6:1:

> Brethren, if a man be overtaken in a fault, ye which are spiritual, restore such an one in the spirit of meekness; considering thyself, lest thou also be tempted.

Here is clear instruction in righteous judgment. First, we see that we have a responsibility to seek to lovingly restore a person who is "overtaken in a fault." The phrase "overtaken in a fault" does not mean that a person has stumbled once, but has fallen prey to a habitual and repetitive failure or sin or character flaw. We are to be patient with other people, not pouncing on every little mistake, but lovingly confronting serious sins and character issues. We should be heavyhearted when we have to judge another person and hold him or her accountable. We should not be eager or happy to do so. If we are, we are acting in a sinful and prideful spirit.

Second, notice this key phrase: "ye which are spiritual." Ouch! That phrase should make every Christian wince and stop in his tracks! God, speaking through the apostle Paul, wanted to force us to inspect our own hearts and souls before we jump in with both feet and confront another Christian. That phrase forces us to ask ourselves: How spiritual am I? Do I have sin in my life? Am I Christlike? Or am I more like a Pharisee, looking for another victim?

Third, what does this passage say that "ye which are spiritual" should do? Does it say, "You who are spiritual should *destroy* such a person in a spirit of pride"? No, it says, "Ye which are spiritual, *restore* such an one in the spirit of meekness"! The carping, faultfinding critic tears down. The spiritual, humble Christian servant seeks to build up and restore.

Now, I am no expert on chickens and chicken coops, but I once visited a chicken coop, and there I saw something very sad and instructive.

41

There were a lot of little chickens in this coop, and one of them had a wound. If you have an idealized view of cute little fuzzy chickens, then you might think that all the other chickens would go to the side of their wounded little friend and would lovingly, considerately try to console him. But that is not what real chickens do. Chickens are pharisaical. If they see a wounded brother, they go to him and peck at his wound. They peck and peck while the wounded chicken cries out in pain. They peck until the wound opens up, and finally the poor bird dies, a victim of his pharisaical brethren. Unfortunately, many Christians act like these chickens.

Fourth, Galatians 6:1 tells us that when we judge another Christian, we must first consider ourselves, lest we be tempted. What temptations do we face? What sins and character flaws do we struggle with? Are we faultless? We must ask ourselves these questions before we attempt to set any other person straight.

We must judge ourselves first, lest we be judged. If we judge ourselves rightly, God will not judge us. But if we judge others pridefully, God will judge us, using the same measuring standard that we have used against our fellow man.

The fact is, Christianity begins with self-judgment. It begins with humility and brokenness and an awareness of one's own sinfulness and wretchedness.

I will never forget the moment when my own Christian experience began—when I first understood what Jesus Christ endured for me, when I truly saw all the sins and evil works I had done, which had been like nails pounded into the flesh of the Son of God. I will never forget the horror I felt when I realized that God—instead of condemning me as I deserved—had placed my sin upon Jesus and had poured out the cauldron of His own wrath upon His beloved Son. Jesus Christ endured pain beyond my ability to imagine, and He endured it because of my own sin!

When I met Christ, when I finally caught a glimpse of what He had really done for me, I saw for the first time what I really was and the sins

I had committed. For the first time in my life, I judged myself and recognized myself as someone I had never known before—the most wicked man on the face of this earth. At that moment, I knew for the first time what it meant to truly be sorry for my sin. And in that revelation of my sin I received a vision of His love and mercy and grace—

And all of that sin was washed away! It was buried in the depths of the sea, never again to be remembered against me. I was washed in the blood of Christ, clothed in the white raiment of His perfect righteousness, faultless to stand before God, covered in Christ's righteousness alone.

If someone had walked in on me at that moment—even the vilest sinner, the most notorious murderer, the worst pornographer or adulterer—I would not have considered myself in any way superior to that person. I was so overwhelmed by my own sin, I didn't have eyes for anyone else's. Oh, that God would give us that spirit of humility and meekness throughout our Christian life! How much more blessed we would be, and how much more of a blessing we would be in the lives of those around us!

To judge or to judge not?

We are commanded to judge, to exercise wisdom and discernment. We are even commanded to confront an erring, sinning brother in a spirit of humility, always judging ourselves first and foremost. But prideful, hypocritical faultfinding is judged and condemned by God.

That is what Jesus taught us when He said, "Judge not, that ye be not judged."

Part II

MYSTERIES OF THE GOSPEL STORY

And [pray] for me, that utterance may be given unto me, that I may open my mouth boldly, to make known the mystery of the gospel.

Ephesians 6:19

You and I will try [to see] if we can throw some little light upon the mystery.

Sir Arthur Conan Doyle
"The Adventure in the Priory School"

THE MYSTERY OF THE VIRGIN BIRTH

I want to assure you right off that I do not believe in the Virgin Birth—and hope that none of you do!"

Those are not my words, I assure you! Those words were spoken in the first half of the twentieth century from the pulpit of the magnificent Riverside Church in New York City. The speaker was the Reverend Harry Emerson Fosdick, leader of the liberal theological movement in America. Those words have echoed throughout liberal churches in America ever since.

Of all the miracles and mysteries of the Bible, the miracle of the Virgin Birth of Jesus Christ has by far come under the fiercest attack. Astoundingly, the most hostile attacks seem to come from those who assert themselves to be theologians and ministers of the Gospel. Claiming to be interested only in stripping away all that is "mythical" and "legendary" about the Gospel story (that is, anything that does not fit their bias of unbelief), they proclaim a so-called "historical Jesus." Their historical Jesus, however, is completely unrecognizable as anyone resembling the Jesus of the New Testament. Their historical Jesus was not born of a virgin. He never healed the sick, never gave sight to the blind, never calmed the storm. He was never resurrected. He was not a Savior. He was just a man.

THE VIRGIN BIRTH: FACT OR FICTION?

This, then, is the next mystery to be solved: Was the Virgin Birth fact—or fiction? Indeed, was the entire Christmas story, as described in the Gospels, an actual event in history or merely a quaint religious legend? Our entire faith depends upon the solution to this mystery.

One prominent enclave of liberal debunkers of the Virgin Birth and other miracles of the Gospels is the so-called Jesus Seminar, founded in 1985 by Robert W. Funk, a religion professor at Vanderbilt University. The stated purpose of the Jesus Seminar is to ignite an "international debate about the 'historical Jesus'—that is, the real facts about the person to whom various Christian gospels refer."[1] According to those who seek the so-called historical Jesus, the Virgin Birth was not an historical fact. It was a work of fiction.

If the Virgin Birth is nothing but fiction, according to the two hundred or so liberal professors and theologians of the Jesus Seminar, then what are the real facts about the historical Jesus? To them, the only real facts are those that portray Jesus as a liberal social activist, just like themselves. In other words, the scholars of the Jesus Seminar have reinvented Jesus in their own image. They strip away everything about Jesus they don't like, that doesn't fit their own self-image as social reformers, and they add a so-called "fifth Gospel" (the heretical, non-canonical, Gnostic Gospel of Thomas, which contains 114 supposed sayings of Jesus, but no miracles, no Virgin Birth, no Resurrection, no claims of salvation). On this basis, the Jesus Seminar has concluded that only 18 percent of the sayings of Jesus recorded in the Bible are authentic. (In the entire Gospel of Mark, they conclude that *only one* statement of Jesus—"Render to Caesar the things that are Caesar's, and to God the things that are God's," Mark 12:17—is authentic!)

Now, these learned scholars and professors have taken a major responsibility upon themselves—the responsibility of judging Holy Scripture, of deciding for the rest of us what is historic truth and what is mere legend and myth, of deleting and disparaging some portions of the Bible while affirming other favorite portions as literally true. In view of this serious burden they have assumed, they certainly must have taken extraordinary steps to ensure that their conclusions are logically, scientifically valid, based on an objective weighing of all the historical and archaeological evidence, right? Wrong.

How have they arrived at their conclusions? By simply taking a vote. They just pool their collective prejudices. All of these liberal-to-radical theologians, most of whom teach in secular universities or liberal seminaries, are given a handful of colored pebbles. A question is put to them: Do you believe Jesus did this, as the Gospels record? Do you believe He said that? Do you believe He was born of a virgin? Do you believe He physically rose from the dead? And they vote with their colored pebbles, and the newspapers, magazines, and broadcast journalists gleefully report their conclusions.

The Jesus Seminar conducts no research. It conducts only polls of liberal scholars. The results are hardly surprising—and certainly not enlightening. The group's pebble-based polls are merely an expression of its collective unbelief. As a result, the Jesus Seminar has decided that the Virgin Birth never occurred, that the visit of the wise men was pure fiction, that the flight into Egypt was a flight of fancy, and that the entire Christmas story is a myth. If you send your sons or daughters to a secular university and they take a course in religion, expect them to come home at Christmastime to report that your family is celebrating a myth. Even though the Jesus Seminar and its allies throughout secular academia haven't a shred of evidence to support their conclusions, thousands are being misled because these scholars are supposedly the "experts."[2]

I recall a class from my seminary days, taught by Dr. William Childs Robinson. At one point, a student challenged a statement that he made, saying, "But Dr. Robinson, the experts say . . ."

"Just a moment," Dr. Robinson interrupted. "The experts say—everything."

That is absolutely true. You can find experts on every side of every issue.

I submit to you that the Jesus of the Gospels is the only historical Jesus. There is no need to take a vote to determine the validity of the Gospels. The historical reliability of the New Testament documents has been verified again and again on the basis of *hard* evidence, not some liberal scholar's imagination and unbelieving prejudice. We know that the New Testament texts have been faithfully transmitted to us from ancient times to today, because we have roughly 25,000 ancient manuscripts available for study (5,686 Greek manuscripts, more than 10,000 in the Latin Vulgate, and some 9,300 other early versions). In contrast, only 643 manuscripts of Homer's *Iliad* (written before 700 B.C.) exist, the earliest complete manuscript being a mere 700 years old (compared with New Testament manuscripts that are nearly 2,000 years old!)[3]

The historical accuracy of the New Testament documents is confirmed by their remarkable agreement with one another; by ancient historians (such as Josephus and Tacitus), who independently reported some of the same events; by early Church fathers (Justin Martyr, Irenaeus, Clement of Alexandria, Origen, Tertullian, Hippolytus, and Eusebius), who affirmed the historical events of the New Testament; and by the testimony of archaeology, which again and again has confirmed the veracity of New Testament reporting. As Dr. Gleason Archer has stated in his *Encyclopedia of Bible Difficulties*:

> As I have dealt with one apparent discrepancy after another and have studied the alleged contradictions between the biblical record and the evidence of linguistics, archaeology, or science, my confidence in the trustworthiness of Scripture has been repeatedly verified and strengthened by the discovery that almost every problem in Scripture that has ever been discovered by man, from ancient times until now, has been dealt with in a completely satisfactory manner by the biblical text itself, or else by objective archaeological information. The deductions that may be validly drawn from ancient Egyptian, Sumerian, or Akkadian documents all harmonize with the biblical record; and no properly trained evangelical scholar has anything to

fear from the hostile arguments and challenges of humanistic rationalists or detractors of any and every persuasion.[4]

So, in our own quest for the historical Jesus, we have a choice: Do we trust the well-attested, historically, and scientifically verified documents of the New Testament—or do we place our trust in the colored-pebble consensus of the radical Jesus Seminar? Do we trust the revealed Word of God—or the imaginations and biases of so-called experts?

Let the liberal theologians and secular historians shut their eyes to the miracle of the virgin's womb and the empty tomb. One day they will be forced to admit that what they have so casually dismissed as legend was history itself. And the One whose glory and majesty they have tried to strip away is no mere man—He is the Christ, and before Him every knee will bow and every tongue confess that He is Lord.

WHAT DIFFERENCE DOES THE
VIRGIN BIRTH MAKE?

The question of the Virgin Birth is no secondary or peripheral matter. It is a central and foundational issue of the Christian faith. The Virgin Birth was prophesied in the Old Testament: "Therefore the Lord himself shall give you a sign; Behold, a virgin shall conceive, and bear a son, and shall call his name Immanuel" (Isa. 7:14). This prophecy was fulfilled in the New Testament:

> And the angel answered and said unto her, The Holy Ghost shall come upon thee, and the power of the Highest shall overshadow thee: therefore also that holy thing which shall be born of thee shall be called the Son of God. (Luke 1:35)

Some people, like the "experts" of the Jesus Seminar, attack this boldly and directly. They simply declare that the Virgin Birth never happened. But others, a more subtle and deceptive variety of skeptic, take the indirect approach. Instead of attacking the Virgin Birth as a myth, they say, "It really doesn't matter whether you believe it or not. Whether Jesus was born of a virgin or not is simply unimportant." Perhaps that statement has even been made in your church.

What difference does the Virgin Birth make? I've thought a lot about this question and came up with this list of the differences that the Virgin Birth makes to our faith:

- If Jesus were not born of a virgin, then the New Testament narratives are false and unreliable.

- If Jesus were not born of a virgin, then Mary is stained with the sin of unchastity. Being betrothed to Joseph was a far more binding matter in Mary's Jewish culture than being engaged is in our own culture. In order to break a betrothal, one had to obtain a bill of divorcement. If unchastity was the grounds for divorcement, the guilty party was not considered to have merely committed fornication, but adultery. In those days, a woman found guilty of adultery was punished by being taken to the gate of the city, where her clothes were ripped and her jewelry removed; she was dressed in rags, tied with a rope, and paraded and made an example to all of the other women of the city, so that they would be warned not to engage in such lewdness. Those who deny the Virgin Birth accuse Mary of adultery.

- If Jesus were not born of a virgin, then He was mistaken about His paternity. Again and again, He declared Himself to be the Son of God, and He declared that God was His Father.

- If Jesus were not born of a virgin, then Christ was not born of the seed of a woman (Gen. 3:15) but of the seed of a man.

- If Jesus were not born of a virgin, then He was not the Son of God, but merely the illegitimate child of a sinful liaison between a Jewish peasant girl and an unknown man.

- If Jesus were not born of a virgin, then He is not the God-man; He is just a man.

- If Jesus were not born of a virgin, then He was just a sinner like the rest of us.

- If Jesus were not born of a virgin, then He cannot be the divine Redeemer, because the sacrifice for sin must be perfect.

- If Jesus were not born of a virgin, we have no Savior.

- If Jesus were not born of a virgin, we are still in our sins and without forgiveness.

- If Jesus were not born of a virgin, we have no hope after death.

- If Jesus were not born of a virgin, there is no mediator between God and man.

- If Jesus were not born of a virgin, there is no Trinity, because there is no Second Person of the Trinity.

- If Jesus were not born of a virgin, Christ should not have prayed, "Father, forgive them," but rather, "Father, forgive us," because He was a sinner just like the rest.

- Lastly, if Jesus were not born of a virgin, if this miracle of the Virgin Birth is denied, where shall we draw the line? What miracle is left? And if there are no miracles, then is there a God? Is there a heaven? Is there a soul? Is there any hope for humanity beyond the grave?

It seems that this miracle, more than any other miracle of the New Testament, sticks in the throats of people who consider themselves liberal Christians. According to one study, 56 percent of seminary students—people who are preparing to become ministers!—do not believe in the Virgin Birth![5]

I would hasten to point out that in the Presbyterian Church in America (PCA), with which I am affiliated, not one minister disbelieves the Virgin Birth. Affirmation of the inerrancy of Scripture and the reality of the Virgin Birth are requirements for ordination as a minister in the PCA. Every minister in my denomination believes in the Virgin Birth, as does every true Christian, in my opinion.

ANTISUPERNATURAL BIAS

Why, then, do so many churches and ministers reject the Virgin Birth? The first reason is a basic antisupernatural bias—a naturalistic frame of mind that refuses to accept the miraculous at all. Clearly, if you don't believe in miracles, you don't believe in the Virgin Birth.

Dr. Manford George Gutzke, one of my seminary professors, used to say that the Virgin Birth is no big problem at all for God. If there is a God who created the universe, if He flung the galaxies from His fingertips, if He frosted the night sky with the scintillating glow of the Milky Way, then it would be a small matter for Him to create a tiny seed and place it in the womb of a young Jewish woman.

Gutzke said that if you can't believe that God can do a little thing like that, then you really don't believe in God at all. If He can't do that, He can't do much of anything. So you see that behind a disbelief in the Virgin Birth lurks the gaping abyss of atheism. The first reason for the rejection of this miracle is a fundamental antisupernatural prejudice that rules the hearts of many, even in the clergy.

THE ARGUMENT FROM SILENCE

The second reason some people reject the Virgin Birth is the so-called "argument from silence." The argument from silence was raised in an interesting encounter between the late Dr. Harry Rimmer, a Presbyterian minister who held doctorates in theology and science, and an older minister on the floor of a presbytery. These two men were examining a young seminary graduate who was a candidate for ordination to the ministry. The young man said he didn't believe in the Virgin

Birth—a statement that caused quite a furor in that presbytery. The older minister stood up and said, "Now, now, let's not make a big deal of this. After all, I am a minister in this presbytery, and I don't believe in the Virgin Birth either."

There was a moment of shocked silence, then someone asked, "Why not?"

"Very simple," said the old minister. "Virgin Birth is only mentioned in two books of the Bible, Matthew and Luke. It doesn't appear at all in Mark or John. Paul never refers to it. Therefore, I don't believe it."

At that point, Dr. Rimmer stood to his feet and said, "Then, sir, what do you preach and teach?"

"Oh," said the old minister, "I preach the Sermon on the Mount. That's enough for anyone."

To which Dr. Rimmer enjoined, "Well, it's not enough for me."

The old minister frowned. "Why not?"

"Because," said Dr. Rimmer, "I don't believe that Jesus ever preached the Sermon on the Mount."

A shocked collective gasp issued all around the room. The old minister was incensed. "For heaven's sake, why not?" he asked.

"Isn't it obvious?" said Dr. Rimmer. "The Sermon on the Mount is only found in two Gospels, Matthew and Luke—the same two Gospels that mention the Virgin Birth of Christ. It is never mentioned by Mark or John. Paul never refers to the Sermon on the Mount in his letters. Therefore, I conclude that Jesus never preached it."

The argument from silence claims that a statement found in one or two Gospels is not valid unless it is also found in the other Gospels or the letters of Paul. So the skeptics try to make a case that if John and Paul are silent on a given subject, then we can't trust Matthew or Luke. But, once we start deleting bits and pieces of Scripture according to our individual biases and whims, where do we stop?

You can carry this argument from silence even further. For example, Mark not only never mentioned the Virgin Birth, he never mentioned the birth of Christ at all! Therefore, any intelligent, sophisticated person would certainly conclude that Mark didn't believe that Jesus was ever born! Not only that, but Paul never mentioned any of the miracles Jesus performed, so Paul obviously didn't believe Jesus worked any miracles. If we follow that line of reasoning, we can remove all of Jesus' miracles from the New Testament.

There's more: Paul never mentioned the parables of Jesus either, and that proves conclusively that Jesus never told any parables!

By now it should be clear that an argument from silence is no argument at all. When Dr. Rimmer made his point about the argument from silence, it was the old minister who was silenced. And so should be any other person who thinks clearly and deeply about the historical meaning of God's Word.

THE VIRGIN BIRTH AND PAGAN MYTHOLOGIES

A third reason many reject the Virgin Birth is that stories of miraculous and virgin births abound in various pagan religions and mythologies. Some claim that the biblical story of the Virgin Birth was plagiarized from these earlier pagan myths. To mention just a few:

- According to Greek mythology, the god Zeus came into Alcmene without sexual relations, producing the virgin-born hero Hercules.

- According to Buddhist legend, the Buddha was born of the virgin Maya.

- Vishnu, in his eighth incarnation, or avatar, emerged as the god Krishna, born of the virgin Devaki.

- Augustus Caesar and Alexander the Great both claimed to be the offspring of virgin births.

So, say the critics and skeptics, the Virgin Birth of Christ was not simply a myth—it was a *stolen* myth, taken from pagan religions. But take a closer look at the quality and credibility of these pagan stories:

- In the case of Zeus fathering Hercules by a virgin, we discover what we commonly find in Greek mythology—that the gods are nothing but men enlarged to god-size, but with all the usual human sins and foibles, cohabiting with human beings. The Greek gods are often depicted as lusting for mortal women.

- As for Buddha, his mother claimed that a six-tusked white elephant with red veins came into her side and caused the Buddha to be conceived.

- In the case of Vishnu, reincarnated as the virgin-born Krishna—according to legend, he had first been incarnated as a fish, a turtle, a boar, a lion, and other bizarre creatures. It is hard to see the correlation between this story and the story of the Virgin Birth of Jesus.

- In the case of Augustus Caesar, he claimed that his mother, Olympia, had been impregnated by a snake; Alexander the Great also made the claim that his father was a snake. (Why this is something to boast about is beyond me!)

What a difference between these depraved and bizarre pagan fantasies and the chaste, pure, dignified record of the Virgin Birth of Christ. The thrust of the skeptic's argument is that these scandalous and repugnant pagan stories antedate the story of the Virgin Birth of Christ, so Matthew and Luke must have stolen them from the earlier pagan sources. But this argument is easily dispelled.

The story of the Virgin Birth was told some seven centuries before Christ—but not by the pagans. No, it is found in the ancient Jewish Scriptures, in Isaiah 7:14, where God says He will give the people a sign: "Behold, a virgin shall conceive, and bear a son, and shall call his name Immanuel." This passage predates almost all of the pagan virgin birth accounts, and its fulfillment by the birth of Christ is cited in Matthew 1:23.

THE PROTEVANGELIUM

But let's go back even farther, and we discover an even older promise of the Virgin Birth. It is found in the passage known as the Protevangelium (from *proto*, meaning "original," and *evangelium*, the Christian Gospel). The Protevangelium is the first Gospel, that wondrous promise God gave to our first parents in Eden. After Adam and Eve were tempted and sinned, the deadly venom of sin entered into the veins of the human race. But even in the midst of that terrible darkness, God lit a candle of hope. We discover the Protevangelium in this verse, where God says to the tempter, the serpent:

> And I will put enmity between thee and the woman, and between thy seed and her seed; it shall bruise thy head, and thou shalt bruise his heel. (Gen. 3:15)

Here we see the Christian Gospel distilled into a single verse in the earliest pages of the first book of the Old Testament. Here God says that the seed of the woman will destroy the head of the serpent, even though the serpent will wound the heel of the seed of the woman. Who is the seed of the woman? Jesus Christ. On the cross, He was slain—but the Resurrection lay ahead of Him. The Cross could not ultimately destroy Him. By dying on the cross, He crushed the head of the serpent, who is Satan. Sin, death, and the devil have all been defeated on the cross.

In all of Scripture, no one but Jesus is referred to as the "seed of the woman." Every other person whose lineage is described is said to be begotten by a man, not a woman. In Scripture, the lineage, or genealogy, is always passed down by the father, not the mother—except in this one verse in Genesis.

In the chronologies of Christ, we read how Abraham begat Isaac, who begat Jacob, who begat so and so, who begat David, who begat so and so, and on and on, until we finally read in Matthew 1:16, "And

Jacob begat Joseph the husband of Mary, of whom [feminine pronoun] was born Jesus, who is called Christ." Jesus Christ was the only human being who was not begotten by man, but born of the seed of a woman. His Father was God. That is the promise of Genesis 3:15, the Protevangelium.

THE ULTIMATE AFFIRMATION

Jesus came into a world where *all* have sinned—yet He lived a sinless life. How is that possible? There is only one explanation: the Virgin Birth! Jesus did not inherit the venom of sin that poisoned the rest of the human race. Why? Because His father was not a man, but almighty God. The perfect sinless life of Christ is the ultimate affirmation of the Virgin Birth.

But there is yet another objective reason for believing in the Virgin Birth: the Resurrection. There is a mountain of evidence that confirms the reality of the Resurrection. That enormous body of evidence takes the issue of Jesus Christ's birth and genealogy out of the realm of subjective speculation and places it firmly in the realm of objective, verifiable proof.

The Resurrection is the most firmly attested event of ancient history. Because we know that Jesus was truly raised from the dead, we know that His birth *must* have been just as miraculous. The Scriptures tell us that when God raised Jesus from the dead, God put His stamp of approval upon the atonement of Jesus Christ—His payment for our sins upon the cross. The Resurrection was God's declaration that Jesus' sacrifice upon the cross was accepted as *payment in full* for our sins. The sacrifice would not have been accepted if Christ were not pure, if He had been a mere sinner like all of us. The Virgin Birth guarantees the purity of the sacrifice of Jesus on the cross.

And His sacrifice guarantees our salvation.

Those who reject the Virgin Birth would tear the heart out of the Christian faith and throw it on the ground. The Virgin Birth is central to salvation, central to Christianity. Without it, Christianity collapses and becomes just another collection of ancient sayings by a long-dead teacher. Without it, everything that is vital and dynamic about the Christian faith crumbles to dust.

Larry King, the master interviewer of the Cable News Network, once appeared as a guest on the *Late Show with David Letterman.* During the course of their conversation, Letterman asked Larry King, "If you could interview any person from history, who would it be?"

Without a moment's hesitation, King responded, "Jesus Christ."

Letterman, who is rarely at a loss for words, looked stunned. It was clearly not the answer he had expected. Making a halting, stammering recovery, Letterman followed up with this question: "Well, what would you ask Him?"

"I would ask Him," replied King, "if He was really born of a virgin. The answer to that question would define history."

At that moment, Letterman truly was at a loss for words! Quietly, he turned to the camera and said, "We'll be right back."

Larry King was right. That question does indeed define history. All of human history is measured from the moment before and the moment after the Virgin Birth. It is the event that was first foretold in the Garden of Eden; it was earnestly awaited and prophesied again and again throughout the Old Testament era; it was foretold in the stars; it took place at a specific time and place in human history; and it continues to reverberate down through the ages, transforming individual lives and entire societies.

How did God accomplish the Virgin Birth? That remains one of the deep mysteries of God's wisdom and power. But did it truly take place? That Bible mystery has been solved for all time. The truth of the Virgin Birth is one of the unshakable cornerstones of our faith—and of our lives.

MORE MYSTERIES OF THE BIRTH OF CHRIST– GENEALOGIES AND PROPHECIES

I f you ever go to France, be sure to visit the great cathedral at Chartres, which was constructed over the course of a century, from 1120 to 1220. The stained glass that adorns the cathedral was fashioned when the art form of illuminated windows was at its height. Those brilliantly colorful transparent mosaics were not designed merely for decoration. Each window is made up of sections called *medallions,* and as you view these medallions in their proper sequence, the window tells a story.

The most renowned and beautiful of all the windows at Chartres is the "Jesse Tree" window, which presents the genealogy of Christ in luminous color. In the exalted position just under the arch of the window is Jesus, and below Him is His mother, Mary. In medallions that surround and support Jesus and Mary are images of kings of Jesus' Davidic bloodline and images of the Old Testament prophets who foretold His coming. The window is called the "Jesse Tree" window because winding through the window are the flowering branches of a beautiful tree—the family tree of Jesse, the father of Israel's King David.

So the Jesse Tree window presents the family tree of Jesus the King—the genealogy of Christ as it is presented in the Gospels. It is a royal lineage, and it is important that we understand and appreciate the kingly genealogy of Christ. Today, we tend to skip over the genealogies of Christ that appear in Matthew and Luke as "filler." But they are not filler. They are included in these two Gospels because they are crucially important aspects of the story of Jesus Christ.

But these two genealogies also present us with a Bible mystery—a mystery that some skeptics and critics have been quick to seize upon to attack the Christian faith. One such critic is noted atheist Dan Barker of the Freedom From Religion Foundation. Writing in the Madison, Wisconsin, *Capital Times* shortly before Christmas 1993, Barker made this observation:

> Modern biblical scholars and theologians distinguish between the "Jesus of history" and the "Christ of faith." . . . In the recently published *The Five Gospels: The Search for the Authentic Words of Jesus*, dozens of eminent Christian scholars [these so-called Christian scholars are all part of the liberal Jesus Seminar we discussed in Mystery 4] conclude that the "Jesus of the Gospels is an imaginative theological construct, into which has been woven traces of that enigmatic sage from Nazareth" . . .
>
> The Gospels are internally contradictory: for example, the differing genealogies of Jesus by Matthew and Luke . . . The "Jesus Christ" of the Gospels, worshiped by most Christians today, is a myth.[1]

So the genealogies of Christ—once viewed as a source of inspiration for the great artistic triumph of the Jesse Tree window at Chartres—are now called "contradictory" by skeptics and atheists like Dan Barker. But are the genealogies of Matthew 1 and Luke 3 contradictory, as the critics claim?

That is the next Bible mystery we will explore. The solution to this mystery provides still more proof of the profound trustworthiness of God's Word.

THE JESUS GENEALOGIES: CONTRADICTORY OR COMPLEMENTARY?

In Matthew 1, the genealogy begins with Abraham and comes down to Christ. In Luke 3, Luke begins with Jesus and works his way back through David and Abraham, all the way up to Adam, who, being directly created by God, is called "the son of God." Matthew, writing primarily for the Jews, traces His Abrahamic and Davidic descent; Luke, writing primarily for Gentiles, traces His descent all the way to Adam, establishing His genetic link to the progenitor of the entire human race.

The main purpose of these genealogies is to prove the Messiahship of Christ. That is done in three ways:

1. The genealogies show that Jesus is a descendant of Abraham. In Genesis 22:18, we read that through the seed of Abraham the whole world would be blessed. In Galatians 3:16, the apostle Paul said that the seed of Abraham was Christ. Jesus was the seed of Abraham who would come into the world and bring the blessings of God upon all the world. The genealogies both show that Jesus was the descendant of Abraham; Matthew 1:2 begins, in fact, with the statement "Abraham begat Isaac."

2. The genealogies show that Jesus was also of the tribe of Judah. This is important, because in Genesis 49:10 we read this prophecy:

> The sceptre shall not depart from Judah, nor a lawgiver from between his feet, until Shiloh come . . .

Shiloh is another name for the Messiah, so this prophecy not only predicts the coming of the Messiah, but states that the Messiah must come before the "scepter" (a term that symbolizes legal authority, sovereignty, and tribal identity) is removed from the tribe of Judah.

Josephus, a noted Jewish general and historian, writing in *Antiquities of the Jews* (20:9), described a most amazing event:

> After the death of the procurator Festus, when Albinus was about to succeed him, the high priest Ananias considered it a favorable opportunity to assemble the Sanhedrin. He therefore caused James, the Brother of Jesus, who was called Christ, and several others, to appear before this hastily assembled council, and pronounced upon them the sentence of death by stoning. All the wise men and strict observers of the law who were at Jerusalem expressed their disapprobation of this act . . . Some even went to Albinus himself, who had departed to Alexandria, to bring this breach of the law under his observation, and to inform him that Ananias had acted illegally in assembling the Sanhedrin without the Roman authority.

Here, Josephus—who was not a Christian—not only affirms the historicity of Jesus and His half-brother James, but also makes note of a crucial historical fact: *The Sanhedrin had no authority to pass a death sentence.* At one time, even during the Roman occupation, the Judaean Jews had retained the right to pronounce judgment and sentence capital cases (what the Romans called the *jus gladii*), but at a certain point in Jewish history, this right—this scepter of authority!—was removed from Judah.

When was the scepter removed from Judah? The Palestinian Talmud (along with the Babylonian Talmud, one of the two ancient collections of Jewish civil and religious law), tells us *exactly* when this power was taken away by the Roman government:

> A little more than forty years before the destruction of the Temple, the power of pronouncing capital sentences was taken away from the Jews.[2]

How did the Jewish leaders view the removal of this power? They viewed it as the negation of God's promise through Jacob to the people of Judah, as recorded in Genesis 49:10. They saw it as the annulment of God's prophecy! Though God had promised that the scepter of power and authority would not depart from Judah until the coming of the Messiah, Rome had deposed Archelaus as king, stripped the scepter from Judaean hands, and placed all power in the hands of the Roman proconsul. The tribe of Judah and the kingdom of Judaea were all that remained of Israel's former greatness—and now even that had been crushed under the Roman heel.

In his book *Jesus Before the Sanhedrin*, Augustin Lemann records a statement by one of the rabbis of that era, describing the reaction of the Jews to this Roman insult to Jewish sovereignty:

> When the members of the Sanhedrin found themselves deprived of their right over life and death, a general consternation took possession of them: they covered their heads with ashes, and their bodies with sackcloth, exclaiming: "Woe unto us, for the scepter has departed from Judah and the Messiah has not come."[3]

Why did the Jews respond with such dismay and horror, putting on sackcloth and ashes? Because they believed that the prophecy of Genesis 49:10 had been voided by the Roman government. The scepter had departed from Judah *and the Messiah had not come*—

Or so they thought!

For while the Jewish leaders in Jerusalem wept and bemoaned the loss of the scepter, a few miles away in the sleepy town of Nazareth, a boy of about eleven or twelve was growing up, the living fulfillment of Jacob's ancient promise to Judah. Jesus of Nazareth, Shiloh, the long-awaited Messiah, had indeed come!

Once the scepter was removed from Judah, it was no longer possible for any Messiah to come at a later date. Today, any Jewish people who still wait for the Messiah are waiting in vain, for the prophecy of Genesis 40:10 is already fulfilled. No other Messiah can come once the scepter is removed.

What's more, the temple of Jerusalem, the place where the genealogical records were kept, was destroyed by Titus and Vespasian in A.D. 70. Today it is no longer possible for any Jew to prove himself to be a descendant of the tribe of Judah—a necessary condition for the Messiah. Clearly, Jesus was Shiloh, the Messiah. He is the one the Jewish people—and all of mankind—have desired and longed for.

3. The genealogies of Matthew and Luke also prove that Jesus was the son of David. This was important because the Old Testament contains many prophecies that identify the Messiah as David's descendant. Isaiah 9:6–7 is just one such messianic prophecy:

> For unto us a child is born, unto us a son is given: and the government shall be upon his shoulder: and his name shall be called Wonderful, Counsellor, The mighty God, The everlasting Father, The Prince of Peace. Of the increase of his government and peace there shall be no end, upon the throne of David, and upon his kingdom, to order it, and to establish it with judgment and with justice from henceforth even for ever. The zeal of the LORD of hosts will perform this.

It was clear to all the Jews that the Messiah would come from the line of David. In Matthew 22:41–42, we read:

> While the Pharisees were gathered together, Jesus asked them, saying, What think ye of Christ? whose son is he? They say unto him, The son of David.

So there is no doubt that the Jews knew that the Messiah must come through the genealogical line of David, nor is there any doubt that Jesus claimed to be the Son of David. If Jesus were not, in fact, descended from David, it would have been a very simple thing for His opponents, the scribes and chief Pharisees, to disprove, because they themselves were the keepers of the genealogical records—records that were carefully stored away in the temple. If Jesus were not descended from David, a few minutes' investigation could have proved Him a fraud—and His enemies certainly would have exposed Him if they could have.

But they couldn't. There is not even a hint in the Gospels or anywhere else that Jesus' claim as a descendant of David was ever challenged. So the genealogical records prove that Jesus is of the seed of Abraham; He is of the tribe of Judah; He is a descendant of David. He fulfills the requirements for the Messiah.

TWO GENEALOGIES, TWO LINEAGES

Now let's consider the problems that accompany these two genealogies in Matthew and Luke. There are differences in the names included in these genealogies, yet they seem to be in both cases the genealogies of Joseph, the stepfather of Jesus. Many have wrestled with these problems and tried to solve them. The solution, however, is actually very simple when you have the key: Matthew lists the genealogy of Joseph, while Luke gives the genealogy of Mary.

Incidentally, it is important to understand that the Jews did not normally include the names of women in their genealogies—yet the genealogy in Matthew names four women: Tamar, Rahab, and Bathsheba (all of whom have stories marred by immorality), plus Ruth, a Gentile. By including the names of these women, God shows us that, by the grace of Jesus Christ, He receives sinners and aliens who were once estranged from the covenant, and He elevates and ennobles the status of women, who were treated as chattel and inferiors in the ancient Middle Eastern cultures.

Now let's solve the mystery of the differing genealogies. First, consider Matthew 1:16: "And Jacob begat Joseph the husband of Mary, of whom was born Jesus, who is called Christ." Here Matthew uses a *periphrasis*, a turning of words. The point I would have you notice is: Who is the father of Joseph? Matthew's answer: The father of Joseph is Jacob.

Next, consider Luke 3:23: "And Jesus himself began to be about thirty years of age, being (as was supposed) the son of Joseph, which was the son of Heli [or Eli]." Here we are told that Joseph is the son of Eli. Unless Joseph had two different fathers, then one of these genealogies cannot be the genealogy of Joseph. What is the solution to this mystery?

Bible scholars will tell you that it is not uncommon in ancient Jewish genealogies, when the lineage of the grandfather passed to a grandson through a daughter, that the name of the daughter was omitted and the daughter's husband was counted as the son of the grandfather. So we see that Jacob was the father of Joseph, who was the legal father (in actuality, the stepfather) of Jesus. Eli was the father of Mary, who was the genetic mother of Jesus. But Joseph is counted as the son of both Jacob and Eli in these two genealogies. In one case, he was the son; in the other case, he was the son-in-law.

Some critics and skeptics have claimed that the Bible does not use language this way, but in Ruth 1, Naomi refers to Ruth, her daughter-in-law, as "my daughter." And in 1 Samuel 24, Saul refers to David, his son-in-law (through marriage to Saul's daughter Michal), as "my son, David." This was a common custom of the Jews.

So it is clear that Matthew gives the genealogy of Joseph, and Luke gives the genealogy of Mary. This should not be interpreted as strange, because it is very clear in the first two chapters of Matthew that Matthew is giving Joseph's story. In fact, he refers to Joseph twenty-eight times. In the first two chapters of Luke, Luke makes scores of references to Mary, including the complete text of Mary's song. So it is only natural that he would give the genealogy of Mary.

Furthermore, if we had two genealogies of Joseph, who was not the genetic father of Jesus but merely the legal father, wouldn't it be strange that his genetic parentage would not be listed for us at all? In fact, as McClintock and Strong note in their *Biblical Encyclopedia* (published in the late 1800s), the Jews called Mary in Hebrew *Bath Heli*, which means "daughter of Eli." She was indeed the daughter of Eli; and

Joseph, her husband, was counted as his son. So the mystery is resolved simply and beautifully in Scripture.

And there is yet more proof that the genealogy in Luke describes the lineage of Mary, not Joseph. In Matthew 1:12, the genealogy of Joseph, we find this statement: "And after they were brought to Babylon, Jechonias begat Salathiel." Who is Jechonias (or Jechoniah)? He was a wicked king described in Jeremiah 22. There he is called Coniah (the name Jechoniah or Je-Coniah is simply a version of his name with the *Je-* prefix appended, which refers to Jehovah). In Jeremiah 22:30, God prophesies that none of Jechoniah's descendants will prosper on the throne of David. Yet, it is through David, his son Solomon, and that royal line (which goes down to Jechoniah) that the Messiah must come!

This would seem to be an unsolvable mystery—if the Messiah's lineage were traced only through Joseph, then the Messiah would be a descendant of Jechoniah, which would violate the prophecy of Jeremiah 22:30. But God had an ingenious plan for unlocking this mystery that no human mind could have foreseen. One branch of the line of David does indeed cut off at Jechoniah—but another branch descends in another direction, through Nathan, bypassing wicked Jechoniah, and coming down through Mary. In this way, the prophecy against Jechoniah is fulfilled. The biological lineage of Jesus does not come through that evil king, but through the Virgin Mary.

If Jesus had not been virgin-born and if the genetic seed of Joseph were in Him, Jesus could not have been the Messiah, because he would have been of the lineage of Jechoniah. God performed a miracle of prophetic fulfillment. Through the lineage of David, Solomon, down through Jechoniah to Joseph, God established for Jesus a legal title to David's throne—but without placing Jesus in Jechoniah's bloodline. Only through Mary, as recorded in Luke, is Jesus the actual, genetic son of David.

The Bible makes it very clear that Jesus was not, in fact, the genetic son of Joseph. Luke wrote, "And Jesus himself began to be about thirty years of age, being (as was supposed) the son of Joseph." Luke inserted the phrase "as was supposed" because he wanted to make clear that Jesus' real father was not Joseph, but God Himself. Jesus was (as He is termed in Greek) the *theantropos*—the God–man. So we have solved the mystery of the two genealogies. The genealogy in Matthew presents Jesus' legal claim as Messiah to David's throne by way of His adoptive father's lineage; the one in Luke presents his birthright as Messiah and heir to David's throne by way of His bloodline through Mary, His birth mother.

A FINAL WORD: JESUS, THE FULFILLMENT OF 333 PROPHECIES

I once had a conversation with a Jewish man who completely disbelieved that the Scriptures were God's revelation to humanity. He was a writer, an educated and articulate man, but he was completely ignorant of the many evidences for the truthfulness of the Christian faith and the Scriptures that reveal this faith. He said the Bible was simply a book written by men, like any other book. "Oh?" I said. "Then permit me to read you some statements about someone in the Bible. I want to see if you can tell me who these statements describe." He agreed, and I flipped through my Bible and read:

> They that hate me without a cause are more than the hairs of mine head. (Ps. 69:4)

> Why do the heathen rage, and the people imagine a vain thing? The kings of the earth set themselves, and the rulers take counsel together, against the LORD, and against his anointed. (Ps. 2:1–2)

> Yea, mine own familiar friend, in whom I trusted, which did eat of my bread, hath lifted up his heel against me. (Ps. 41:9)

> Smite the shepherd, and the sheep shall be scattered. (Zech. 13:7)

And I said unto them, If ye think good, give me my price; and if not, forbear. So they weighed for my price thirty pieces of silver. And the LORD said unto me, Cast it unto the potter: a goodly price that I was prised at of them. And I took the thirty pieces of silver, and cast them to the potter in the house of the LORD. (Zech. 11:12–13)

They shall smite the judge of Israel with a rod upon the cheek. (Mic. 5:1)

My God, my God, why hast thou forsaken me? . . . All they that see me laugh me to scorn: they shoot out the lip, they shake the head, saying, He trusted on the LORD that he would deliver him: let him deliver him, seeing he delighted in him . . . I am poured out like water, and all my bones are out of joint: my heart is like wax; it is melted in the midst of my bowels. My strength is dried up like a potsherd; and my tongue cleaveth to my jaws . . . For dogs have compassed me: the assembly of the wicked have inclosed me: they pierced my hands and my feet. I may tell all my bones: they look and stare upon me. They part my garments among them, and cast lots upon my vesture. (Ps. 22:1, 7–8, 14–18)

They gave me also gall for my meat; and in my thirst they gave me vinegar to drink. (Ps. 69:21)

Surely he hath borne our griefs, and carried our sorrows: yet we did esteem him stricken, smitten of God, and afflicted. But he was wounded for our transgressions, he was bruised for our iniquities: the chastisement of our peace was upon him; and with his stripes we are healed. (Isa. 53:4–5)

I read all these verses to him and several more. Then I said to him, "About whom did I just read?"

"That's obvious," he replied. "You were reading about Jesus of

Nazareth. Those were verses about His life and ministry, and about His suffering, death, and resurrection."

"Is there any question in your mind about that?"

"No," he answered, "those verses couldn't refer to anyone else but Jesus. What's your point?"

"My point is simply this," I said. "Every one of the verses I just read to you, which you yourself say referred to Jesus, was taken from the Old Testament. The latest book in the Old Testament was written some four hundred years before Jesus was born. Not even the harshest critics of the Bible would ever claim that those verses were written after His birth, because historians know that the entire Old Testament was translated from Hebrew into Greek in Alexandria a century and a half before He was born. Now, if the Bible is merely a book written by men, would you please explain to me how those prophetic passages about Jesus came to be written hundreds of years *before* He was born?"

"I haven't the faintest idea," he replied. His agnostic, humanistic worldview could not explain the profoundly accurate prophecies of Christ contained in the Old Testament.

No other person in history has ever been the subject of so much prophetic writing. You will find no predictive prophecies whatsoever in the writings of the Buddha, Confucius, Muhammad, Lao-tse, or Hinduism. Yet the Old Testament alone contains well over two thousand prophecies, most of which have already been fulfilled. Of these prophecies in the Old Testament, 333 texts deal with the promised Messiah; they contain 456 specific details of His life—456 specific ways in which the Messiah could be identified at His coming to Israel. One of God's purposes in giving the Old Testament to the Jewish people was to bring forth the Messiah from among them and to identify Him to them when He arrived. Those prophecies are so specific in nature that they burn all the bridges behind them. Had they not been fulfilled, there would be room for excuse. How can they possibly be explained in terms of naturalistic, humanistic presuppositions? They can't!

Of all the attacks that have ever been made upon the Scripture, there has never been, to my knowledge, one book written by a skeptic to disprove all the prophecies of Scripture. Though the Bible has been attacked at every other place, the one place where God rests the proof of His inspired Word and the credentials of His Son, Jesus, is on the prophecies of Jesus, which have infallibly come to pass.

Fred John Meldau, author of *Messiah in Both Testaments,* has pointed out that as few as five points of identification can single out any individual from all the billions of human beings on the planet. If someone, anywhere in the world, were to write on an envelope your name, street address, city, state, and nation of residence, that envelope would get to you based on those five points of identification. If the envelope said "U.S.A.," it would single out your location from more than 200 nations on the planet. If it listed your state, it would further single you out from among fifty states in the United States. The city would further narrow it down to a given locality. The address and street name would narrow it down to a single house. And the name would identify the person in that house to whom the letter is addressed.

The Scriptures identify Jesus as the Messiah not by five points of identification, or a dozen, or a hundred, but by 456 specific points of identification in 333 specific Old Testament texts. Does any doubt remain as to His origin and his identity? None whatsoever!

So, in this chapter and the preceding one, we have solved the mysteries surrounding the Virgin Birth, the genealogies of Jesus, and His identity. But the game is yet afoot! There are more deep and exciting mysteries to explore in the life of Jesus Christ. Come! Turn the page with me! Let us examine the profound and endlessly fascinating mysteries of our Lord's death and resurrection.

MYSTERIES OF THE DEATH AND RESURRECTION OF CHRIST

I am about to describe to you a conversation I once had with an American president. Over the course of a lifetime we all have many conversations—thousands of them, in fact—and the vast majority of them fade from memory within days or weeks, if not hours. But some conversations so etch themselves in our minds that we will remember them until the day we die. The conversation I'm about to describe is one such encounter.

I was sitting in a room and across from me, about ten feet away, was seated the then-governor of California and soon-to-be president of the United States, Ronald Reagan. I had the opportunity to ask him some questions. I said, "Governor, I would like to ask you a very important spiritual question: If something were to happen to you and you were to die and stand before almighty God, and He said to you, 'Why should I let you into my heaven?' what would you say?"

His response was surprising. He doubled over, put his head down between his knees and stayed there for some time. Then, after about thirty seconds, he slowly straightened in his chair, looked me in the eye, and in a very sober tone said, "I don't deserve to go to heaven. The only thing that I could say would be, 'For God so loved the world, that he gave his only begotten Son, that whosoever believeth in him should not perish, but have everlasting life'" (John 3:16).

Over the years I have told that story a number of times to various individuals and audiences. I haven't always told it exactly the same way. On some occasions I might have told it this way:

In 1980, I was invited to speak to a man who was one of the leading candidates for president of the United States. I was one of five, maybe six, ministers invited to meet with the candidate as representatives of the evangelical Christian movement in America. Some of the other ministers asked the candidate various questions. When my turn came, I said to him, "Governor, if you were to die and stand before God and He were to say to you, 'Why should I let you into my heaven?' what would you say?"

Now, let me stop right there. What have I just done? I have told the same story twice—but I have told it in two ways. The first version contained more drama, but omitted some details contained in the second version. These two versions of the same story were substantially different—but did I contradict myself? Was one version true and the other false? No. Both stories were perfectly accurate accounts. The two versions do not contradict each other, but complement each other.

I could have chosen other details to include—the location of the meeting place, the fact that two Reagan aides stood near the door during the discussion, the time of year and the weather—but I didn't. We all tell stories, and in the process we choose some details to supplement the account, to heighten the drama, or to make a point; and we omit other details for the sake of simplicity or clarity or because we simply forgot to mention them. The fact that we might tell the same story in different ways at different times does not negate the truth of the story. We should not mistake complementary and supplementary detail for contradiction or discrepancy.

The New Testament contains several versions of the resurrection of Christ. There are differences in details between these stories. Some skeptics have claimed that these differences constitute contradictions. In fact, in the whole Bible, the Resurrection story contains the largest concentration of facts and details that have been claimed by Bible critics to be contradictions.

Because the Resurrection story is the central story and crucial issue of the entire Christian Gospel, it is important that we solve any mysteries surrounding the death and resurrection of Christ. By facing these mysteries squarely and openly, our faith in the reliability of God's Word is not diminished—it deepens and grows.

THE CASE OF THE VANISHING CONTRADICTIONS

There are numerous small mysteries surrounding the death and resurrection of Jesus Christ. Those who oppose the Christian faith delight in trying to stump believers with such questions as:

- Why does Matthew 27:9–10 quote a verse from Zechariah but attribute it to Jeremiah?

- If Jesus was crucified on Friday and raised on Sunday, how could He have been in the grave for three days?

- Wasn't Jesus mistaken when He promised that the people of His own time would be alive to see the end of the world?

These so-called mysteries are easily solved when you understand the times and customs of the culture to which the Bible was written. For example, when Matthew 27:9–10 quotes from Old Testament prophecies that predicted our Lord's betrayal by a friend for thirty pieces of silver, the writer followed a common practice of that time— merging several Old Testament passages into a single citation. Matthew quoted from Zechariah 11:12–13, as well as from Jeremiah 19:1–3 and 32:6–9, and attributed the entire passage to the major prophet Jeremiah. This was a common practice in those days, and we see another example in Mark 1:2–3, which quotes Malachi 3:1 and Isaiah 40:3 together, but cites only the major prophet Isaiah.

What about the fact that Jesus was not in the grave for three full days, since He was crucified on Friday and raised on Sunday? Again, this is a case of modern critics applying modern standards to an ancient culture and completely missing the point. In such places as Matthew 16:21; 17:23; and 20:19, where Jesus predicted His death and resurrection, He did not claim He would be in the tomb for three full days. He claimed simply that "the third day He will rise again." Jesus was crucified and buried on Friday, remained in the earth on the Sabbath day, and rose again on Sunday, the first day of the week—"the third day." There is no contradiction here, except in the imaginations of hostile critics.

And what of the so-called mystery of Matthew 24:34, where Jesus promised, "This generation shall not pass, till all these things be fulfilled." Critics assume that "this generation" refers to the people who were gathered around Jesus as He spoke. Clearly, this is not what Jesus meant. There are two possible meanings for the term "this generation." In the original Greek, the term generation (genea) could easily mean "race"—a reference to the Jewish race and nation. God had made promises to the nation of Israel, some conditional, some unconditional, including an eternal inheritance of the land of Palestine and the kingdom of David (Gen. 12; 14; 15; 17; 2 Sam. 7). So Jesus may have been referring to God's preservation of the Jewish people in order to fulfill God's promises to Israel. This view is supported by Paul's reference to a time when Israel will be restored to God's covenantal promise (Rom. 11:11–26).

Another view is that Jesus was referring to the generation that would be alive to witness the events which He prophesied. In other words, the same generation that would see the things He described (such as the abomination of desolation, Matt. 24:15, and the time of great tribulation, Matt. 24:30), would also see the judgment of God accomplished. In any event, the critics are clearly wrong in assuming that when Jesus said "this generation," He was literally pointing His finger at the people who were listening to His words. Neither Scripture nor common sense supports such a view.

These simple, commonsense solutions to such commonly cited Bible mysteries show us that God's Word is reasonable and reliable. This is an important foundation as we approach the mysteries we find in the story of the resurrection of our Lord. Those who claim to find contradictions in the Resurrection story often cite one or more of the mysteries we are about to explore. After you examine the evidence, you will see that these mysteries are as easily resolved as the ones we have already examined.

HOW MANY WOMEN WENT TO THE TOMB?

Matthew 28:1–10 tells us that "Mary Magdalene and the other Mary" went to see the tomb. Mark 16:1–8 mentions Mary Magdalene, Mary the mother of James, and Salome. Luke 24 names Mary Magdalene, Mary the mother of James, and Joanna. John 20:1–18 only mentions Mary Magdalene. So from these accounts we glean that at least four women went to the tomb for the purpose of anointing the body of Jesus Christ early on Sunday morning. Those women were Mary Magdalene, Mary the mother of James (probably the "other Mary" mentioned by Matthew), Salome, and Joanna.

Is there a contradiction in these accounts? A critic would say yes. He would seize on the fact that John mentions only Mary Magdalene, while the other writers mention her and other women going to the tomb together, and he would call this a contradiction. But the skeptic's position is very shaky. None of the Gospel writers says, "These are the only women who went to the tomb." John does not say that Mary Magdalene went alone. He only says that she went.

When I told the story of meeting with Reagan, I first told it without mentioning anyone else in the room, then I retold it, mentioning the other participants in that meeting. That is not a contradiction. I merely selected some details and omitted others in the two accounts.

There is no question in my mind but that this is exactly the situation we have between these different accounts in the four Gospels.

A second contradiction skeptics claim to find in this story is the time at which the women came to the tomb.

WHEN DID THE WOMEN GO TO THE TOMB?

According to skeptics, the accounts in John and Mark contradict each other because Mark says that the women came to the grave at sunrise, while John says that Mary Magdalene came to the grave when it was still dark. Now, was the sun rising—or was it still dark? "Gotcha!" say the critics. "Here's a Bible contradiction—time to discard your Christian faith!"

Not so fast. Keep in mind that Mary Magdalene, the apparent leader of this group of women, had to leave her home, walk to the house (or houses) where the other women were staying, gather them together, then go out to the place where the tomb was, outside the city walls of Jerusalem. If the women planned on being there at sunup, they would have to start at least thirty minutes before sunrise, while it was still dark. So John was talking about the time of Mary's *departure* from her home to go to the tomb. Mark, however, was describing the time of the women's *arrival* at the tomb. What seems to be a discrepancy is just a difference in detail selection. We do this kind of thing all the time in our own everyday conversations. Thus, quite simply and easily, another so-called contradiction vanishes into thin air.

Next, critics claim to find a contradiction regarding the angels who appear in the Resurrection account.

HOW MANY ANGELS WERE AT THE TOMB?

In Matthew and Mark, we read that an angel spoke to the women about the resurrection of Jesus. But Luke and John each say there were two angels. Which is it—one angel or two?

Question: Did any of the writers say there was *only* one angel? No. If there were two angels, then obviously there was one angel, plus one more. So to say that an angel was present is not to say that only one angel was present—there might have been another angel. I think it is safe to assume that two of these accounts—Matthew and Mark—do not mention the additional angel because only one of the angels spoke. Matthew and Mark were more focused on presenting the dialogue with the angel who spoke than to detail how many angels were present. To Matthew and Mark, mentioning the angel who did not speak probably seemed as superfluous as, in my story, mentioning the two Reagan aides who stood by the door and did not speak. If it seems to be an unimportant detail, why mention it? Once again, a supposed contradiction vanishes.

"WOMAN, WHY ARE YOU WEEPING?"

In John's account, it seems that Jesus appears to Mary at the tomb. In Matthew, it seems that Jesus appears to the women as they are going to tell the disciples. Is this a contradiction? No. The sequence of events described by the four Resurrection accounts can easily be harmonized in this way:

Mary Magdalene, upon approaching the tomb with the other women, saw that the stone was rolled away. Hearing the angel announce the resurrection of the Lord, she immediately left to tell the disciples the good news. Meanwhile, the angel told the other women, "Fear not ye: for I know that ye seek Jesus, which was crucified. He is not here: for he is risen, as he said. Come, see the place where the Lord lay" (Matt. 28:5–6). And those women did as the angel said, entering the tomb and finding the empty grave clothes where Jesus had been laid to rest. The angel also told the women (v. 7), "And go quickly, and tell his disciples that he is risen from the dead." And they did as the angel said—they left the tomb and went back into the city.

In due time, Mary Magdalene returned to the tomb, and she remained there. Mary's love for her Lord was so great that she could not bring herself to abandon the tomb where His body had been placed, even though He was no longer there. While she was there, she saw a Man that she thought was the gardener. Though she didn't realize it at first, it was Jesus Himself. And John proceeds to give us an intimate, dramatic depiction of the tender dialogue between Jesus and Mary Magdalene.

There is no contradiction between John's narrative and that of the other Gospels, including Matthew's. The other women had already left the tomb, and their encounter with the risen Lord is described in Matthew's Gospel. But John's focus is different from Matthew's, so the events and details he selects are different from Matthew's—different, but not contradictory.

Now, at this point, I want to underscore something that Jesus did toward Mary Magdalene in this passage. He said one word to her that is very significant: *Woman*. John 20:15 records that He said, "*Woman*, why weepest thou?" (emphasis added). Why do I say that this one word is so significant? Because I believe that Jesus Christ has done more to elevate and ennoble the state of women than any other human being who ever lived. The modern feminists have their icons, people from the history of the women's movement that they claim have raised the status of their gender. Yet nowhere in the pantheon of women's champions and martyrs do they list Jesus Christ—but they should!

In all of history, no one has done more than Jesus to champion the cause of women. He restored the dignity of the fallen Samaritan woman He met at the well at Sychar (John 4). Then He spared the life of another woman caught in adultery, and he showed her a lifestyle of righteousness (John 8).

Finally, He liberated yet a third woman who had been demon-possessed, and He healed the pain and sorrow in that woman's aching heart (Mark 16:9; Luke 8:2). That woman's name was Mary Magdalene. Following the Resurrection, Jesus paid her the high honor of revealing Himself to her and speaking to her before He appeared to any other person (John 20:10–18). Mary Magdalene is symbolic of all women everywhere, for women of every culture have much for which to thank Jesus.

By harmonizing the accounts of the four Gospels, the book of Acts, and the statements of the apostle Paul in 1 Corinthians 15, we find that the order of the appearances of the risen Christ to His followers was probably as follows:

1. He appeared first to Mary Magdalene (John 20:10–18), who saw and heard Him when she returned to the empty tomb.

2. Next, He appeared to the other women who had been with Mary at the tomb. This appearance took place as the women were on their way back to their homes. They were going to tell the disciples about the empty tomb when Jesus appeared to them and greeted them, and they worshiped Him (Matt. 28:9–10).

3. Peter was probably the next person to witness the risen Lord (1 Cor. 15:5).

4. Next were the two disciples on the road to Emmaus (Luke 24:13–35). Like Mary Magdalene, they did not recognize Him on sight. Only after hearing Him speak for some time, reminding them of the Old Testament prophecies about Himself, and blessing and breaking bread with them, were their eyes opened to see Him as He was. The very instant they recognized Him, He was taken from their sight.

5. He next appeared to the apostles in the upper room, all except Thomas, the one who doubted (Luke 24:36–49; John 20:19–23).

6. Eight days later, He appeared to all the apostles, including Thomas, in that same upper room (John 20:24–31).

7. Jesus appeared to seven apostles who had been fishing on the Sea of Tiberias. One of them was Peter, whom He commissioned with the command, "Feed my sheep" (John 21).

8. Jesus appeared to all the apostles on a mountain in Galilee, and there He gave them the Great Commission to go and evangelize all nations (Matt. 28:16–20).

9. He also appeared to five hundred Christian believers in one place (1 Cor. 15:6); Paul had apparently spoken with many of these believers and had confirmed their eyewitness accounts.

10. Jesus also appeared to His half brother James (1 Cor. 15:7).

11. After appearing to many witnesses for a period of forty days following the Resurrection, He appeared one last time to all the apostles in Jerusalem, commissioning them as His witnesses in Jerusalem, in all Judaea, and out into Samaria, and unto the farthest reaches of the planet (Acts 1:4–8).

12. Finally, He appeared to a Jewish Pharisee, an enemy of Christ named Saul, on the road to Damascus (Acts 9:1–9; 1 Corinthians 15:8). This man, following his conversion to Christ, became the most effective Christian missionary of the first century A.D.—the apostle Paul.

THE RESURRECTION EVENT

Another supposed contradiction sometimes raised by critics is found in Mark 16:7–8. In verse 7, the angel tells the women who came to the tomb, "But go your way, tell his disciples and Peter that he goeth before you into Galilee." But in verse 8, the writer records that the women went away and "neither said they any thing to any man; for they were afraid."

Now, did the women disobey God's command delivered to them by the angel? That is inconceivable! How, then, could they obey the command and tell the disciples of the Resurrection while at the same time say nothing to anyone because of their fear?

There is no real mystery here unless you approach the Scriptures from a standpoint of hostility and rejection. Clearly, the women fulfilled

God's command to go and tell the disciples—but then they went home and bolted their doors. They didn't go door to door and preach the good news to everyone they met. They didn't shout, "The Lord is risen from the dead!" from their rooftops.

These women did exactly as they were commanded: They told the disciples, but no one else. Why? Because they were terrified! They had seen an angel of God! They had seen a miracle—a stone that was rolled away, an empty tomb, and grave clothes that no longer bound a dead body. And, as Matthew 28:9–10 records, they even saw the living, risen Christ. They weren't ready to get into debates about what had happened that morning. They went home and tried to settle their hearts and recover their wits before speaking to anyone of the marvels and wonders they had seen.

DIFFERING ACCOUNTS OF JUDAS'S DEATH

Another common point of attack by Bible critics involves the accounts of the death of Judas Iscariot in Matthew 27:3–5 and Acts 1:18. Matthew says that Judas hung himself; Acts says that Judas fell headlong and "burst asunder in the midst, and all his bowels gushed out." Though critics continue to raise this as a Bible mystery or contradiction, Bible scholars through the ages have always understood that neither of these accounts excludes the other. They are easily harmonized once you understand the facts. Let us first, however, look at the discrepancy involved with the place where Judas hung himself.

Both Matthew and Acts say that the money Judas was paid to betray Christ was used to purchase "the potter's field" as a burial place for strangers. In Acts 1:18, Peter said "this man purchased a field with the reward of iniquity." Matthew 27:7–8 says that Judas threw the bribe money at the feet of the chief priests who had paid him, and being unwilling to put blood money into the Temple treasury, they purchased the field. Critics call this a discrepancy, but the fact is that the original Greek verb for "purchased" in Acts 1:18, *ktaomai*, has a form which means "to cause the purchase" or "to provide for the purchase." So Judas, by the act of throwing down the blood money in the Temple, provided for the purchase of the potter's field, which became known thereafter as Akel Dama, the Field of Blood.

You can visit the Field of Blood today (its modern name is Hak Ed-Damm). It is a level terrace area beneath the prospect of the southern bluff of the valley of Hinnom. According to tradition, Judas hanged himself from one of the many trees that project over that precipice; he would have probably had to climb out onto a branch, throw himself off with the rope tied about his neck—and then the weight of his body and the force of the fall would have caused the limb to snap, sending him plunging headlong to the jagged rocks at the foot of the bluff. So it is not hard at all hard to imagine how a man could both hang himself and "burst open in the middle," as these accounts describe.

EVIDENCE OF THE RESURRECTION

The third president of the United States, Thomas Jefferson, was so offended by the resurrection of Jesus and the other miracles in the Bible that he took a pair of scissors and cut them out of his Bible. His mutilated Bible was later published as *The Jefferson Bible*. Liberal theologian Rudolf Bultmann was equally offended by the miraculous in Scripture. He once said that no one who uses modern technological conveniences such as a radio or electric lights should be asked to believe in the ancient myths of the Bible, such as the Resurrection, in order to become a Christian.[1]

But the Bible does not give Christians the option of disregarding the miracle of the Resurrection. As the apostle Paul wrote in 1 Corinthians 15:14 and 17:

> And if Christ be not risen, then is our preaching vain, and your faith is also vain . . . And if Christ be not raised, your faith is vain; ye are yet in your sins.

If the Resurrection is a myth or a hoax, Christianity collapses. But what does the evidence say? It demonstrates that the resurrection of Jesus Christ was an historical event, verifiable and real. In fact, the body of evidence for the Resurrection is so strong that the really difficult task is not proving that it took place, but proving that it didn't!

The New Testament does not shy away from rational inquiry but invites it. It offers evidence and talks about proof. Though Jesus told doubting Thomas, "Blessed are they that have not seen, and yet have believed" (John 20:29), He nevertheless invited Thomas to investigate the physical evidence of the Resurrection—the nail prints in His hands, the wound in His side. And He makes the same invitation to us today. If you believe in the Resurrection without requiring proof, you are blessed; but if you need proof, the proof is there and awaiting your inspection. The proof of the Resurrection can be determined by asking a series of questions:

1. *How do we know what we know about the Resurrection?* The New Testament is the primary source of historical information about Jesus and the Resurrection. As I have already mentioned, the New Testament documents have proven again and again to be sound, reliable, and historically accurate. Archaeologists and historians who study non-Bible sources such as ruins, ancient documents, and artifacts, have vindicated the historical accuracy of the Old and New Testaments.

Historians once questioned the accuracy of the account of Pontius Pilate's role in the crucifixion of Jesus. According to the New Testament, Pilate found nothing wrong with Jesus, but the Jewish leaders pressured Pilate and said that if he refused to crucify Jesus, he was not Caesar's friend (John 19:12). So Pilate gave in to their demands. Some historians claimed that this action would have been out of character for a cruel and dominating man like Pilate. But historians later discovered that Pilate had been appointed by a man named Sejanus, who was executed for plotting against Caesar, along with many of those Sejanus had appointed. So Pilate, being a protégé of the disgraced Sejanus, was on thin ice with Rome and in no position to stand up against Caesar. The Jewish leaders had Pilate behind the eight ball: If news of a Palestinian rebellion reached Rome, Pilate's head would have rolled. The New Testament account was confirmed as accurate. Not long after, Pilate was recalled and banished.

Another example: The four Gospels were all written in the first century, within two to five decades of the crucifixion of Jesus. The first three Gospels are dated between A.D. 50–65 and the Gospel of John around A.D. 80–95. But some historians doubted the first-century dating of the Gospel of John, claiming it was written much later—and by someone other than John. The Gospel of John, they claimed, was a forgery, not an eyewitness account. As evidence, they cited the "fact" that the author had gotten a number of geographical details "wrong," and had apparently invented places in Jerusalem that did not actually exist. However, recent archaeological finds reveal that the author of John was right about such once-doubted sites as the Pool of Bethesda (John 5:1), The Pavement (John 19:13), and Jacob's well (John 4). Because the city was demolished by the Roman army of Titus in A.D. 70, a later writer would not have known of such places—but John knew because he was there before the city was destroyed. More evidence for an early authorship of John came to light with the discovery in Egypt of the Ryland's papyrus fragment, containing John 18:31–33, which has been dated as early as A.D. 115, not A.D. 250 as skeptics had said. All similar attempts to undermine the credibility of John's Gospel have failed.[2]

The Gospel of Luke is also validated by history and archaeology. It records that the ministries of John the Baptist and Jesus occurred during the "reign of Tiberius Caesar—Pontius Pilate being governor of Judaea" (Luke 3:1). This statement is verified by the Roman historian Tacitus (A.D. 55–117): "Christ had been executed in Tiberius' reign by the governor of Judaea, Pontius Pilate." A similar finding about the way the Roman government conducted its census has demolished the claim that Luke was wrong about the census in Luke 2. These are just a few examples of the many ways that the historical accuracy of the four

Gospels—Matthew, Mark, Luke, and John—has been confirmed by history and archaeology.

The text of the New Testament is far more well-established and verified than the works of Plato, Aristotle, Herodotus, and other ancient writers, the content of which is never seriously questioned. If there is no reason to question those works, there is even less reason to question the text of the New Testament.

2. What evidence for the Resurrection does the New Testament present? No serious historian doubts that Jesus lived, that His life impacted history, and that He was crucified on a Roman cross outside of Jerusalem in A.D. 30. The Christian claim goes much further than that—Jesus not only died, but He was also resurrected.

The implications of the Resurrection claim are immense, because no mere human being could do that of his own power. The rationale for this claim of Jesus is that He was not a mere human being—He was God in the flesh. If He arose again, as the New Testament claims, then His claim to be God incarnate is valid. If He did not rise again, then the Christian story is a fairy tale and unworthy of the slightest heed by intelligent people.

There have been many attempts by skeptics to discredit the Resurrection story, but none of these attempts is able to account for or explain away the evidence.

Here is the sequence of events: After Christ's torture and crucifixion, His dead body was removed from the cross and bound in linen cloths with about a hundred pounds of burial spices (John 19:39 and following). According to Jewish burial custom, the face was wound with a suffocating combination of cloth and spices. Anyone who thinks there was any chance Jesus could have survived both crucifixion and burial does not understand what the burial was like.

The body was laid in a newly carved-out tomb (a man-made cave in the side of a hill), and a large stone was rolled in front of the opening. The Jewish leaders, remembering Jesus' prediction that He would rise from the dead, asked Pilate to provide a guard (Matt. 27:62–66).

This guard was a detachment of four to sixteen armed Roman soldiers. We know from historical evidence that death was the punishment for such a soldier falling asleep on duty.

Despite all of these precautions, on Sunday morning following the crucifixion, Jesus' tomb was found empty. This fact is recorded in all four Gospels: Matthew 28:6; Mark 16:6; Luke 24:5 and following; John 20:2.

The fact of the empty tomb caused an enormous stir in Palestine. We know this not only from the New Testament evidence, but also from historical evidence. For example, an ancient decree of Claudius Caesar (who reigned A.D. 41–54) was found by archaeologists in Nazareth. It reads, "It is my pleasure that graves and tombs remain perpetually undisturbed . . . In case of violation I desire that the offender be sentenced to capital punishment on charge of violation of sepulchre." Historians believe that the unusual step of decreeing the death penalty for grave robbing is a reaction to the empty tomb of Jesus. The entire Roman empire was turned upside down by the Christian religion, and Claudius did not want any other "resurrection religions" springing up and stirring up trouble.

The Resurrection is the central issue of the Christian faith. All four Gospels describe Jesus' appearances to the disciples after His crucifixion. Luke spoke of the post-Resurrection appearances as a matter of empirical proof: "To whom also he shewed himself alive after his passion by many infallible proofs, being seen of them forty days, and speaking of the things pertaining to the kingdom of God" (Acts 1:3).

Paul, in a letter written about twenty-six years after the crucifixion, records a list of post-resurrection appearances of Christ (1 Cor. 15:3–8). This passage by Paul is considered by scholars to be a recitation of an early Aramaic Christian creed, which was probably formulated within a few years of Jesus' death and resurrection. From the very beginning, from the earliest days of Christianity, the Resurrection was the core issue of the faith.

The Roman historian Tacitus recorded, "But in spite of this temporary setback [the crucifixion] the deadly superstition [Christianity] had broken out afresh, not only in Judaea, where it had started, but even in Rome." Why did this religion spread so quickly and so far? How does one explain the wildfire spread of the Christian faith from a tiny backwater of the Roman Empire to the heart of Rome itself?

It is important to understand what happened to Jesus' disciples in the days following the crucifixion. At first, they were totally disillusioned and scattered. Most of them deserted Jesus when He was arrested, and all but John deserted Him during the crucifixion itself. Afterward, they believed their cause was lost. Then, three days after the death of their Master, these disciples began preaching that Jesus had risen from the dead. We see this intense preaching activity recorded in Acts 2:22–36; 3:12–15; and 10:34–43, and it is all focused on the Resurrection. Nonbiblical sources agree with the New Testament. Josephus wrote, "They reported that he had appeared to them three days after his crucifixion and that he was alive."

It is important to realize where this preaching began: in the city of Jerusalem and the region nearby (Acts 2). This is precisely where Jesus was crucified and buried. The burial tomb belonged to Joseph of Arimathea, a well-known and prominent member of the Jewish ruling council, the Sanhedrin. His tomb was a well-known and easily identified site. Any skeptic who heard the disciples preach about the resurrected Jesus could simply take a fifteen-minute stroll to the tomb and inspect it for himself to see whether it was empty. If the tomb was sealed shut, the disciples would have been laughed out of town. But they weren't laughed at. People believed them, and the Christian faith spread like a life-giving epidemic. Why? Because the *physical evidence*— the empty tomb—was right there at the edge of town, open for inspection.

The Christian movement grew rapidly despite intense persecution from both the Jewish religious leaders and the Roman government. Tacitus described incredible, hideous persecutions inflicted on the early Christians. Those persecutions are also mentioned by Suetonius (secretary to emperor Hadrian, A.D. 117–138) and Pliny the Younger

(Roman historian, A.D. 112). And the strongest proof of all was the courage of the disciples in risking torture and death for the sake of the story of the Resurrection.

Let's suppose that the Resurrection was nothing more than a hoax perpetrated by the disciples. Would they really have been willing to suffer persecution, torture, and death for the sake of a hoax? People might die for a lie if they didn't know it was a lie—but no one would knowingly risk martyrdom for what they *knew* to be a lie!

History records that all of the original disciples were martyred except John, who was banished to the island of Patmos. Luke described the killing of James, the apostle, in Acts 12:2. Josephus told of the stoning of James the Just. The deaths of Peter and Paul were recounted in a letter of an early church father, Clement, to the church in Corinth in about A.D. 95. Peter was crucified upside-down in Rome, and Paul was beheaded. One thing is certain: The Resurrection was not a hoax.

3. What are the skeptical objections to the Resurrection—and how valid are they? Some skeptics insist that miracles are simply not possible. But this is merely an atheistic assumption, a false form of reasoning called an *a priori* conclusion, closing one's mind before even examining the evidence. It is not logical to conclude that miracles are impossible. Once the existence of God is admitted as a possibility, then the possibility of miracles becomes a given. So that objection fails.

Next, skeptics theorize that the body of Jesus was stolen, so the Resurrection was a hoax. This is actually the oldest theory concocted to explain away the Resurrection, and it is recorded in Matthew 28:11–15. There, the soldiers guarding the tomb are bribed by the chief priests and instructed to spread a lie: "Say ye, His disciples came by night, and stole him away while we slept" (Matt. 28:13). This story is so obviously untenable that Matthew doesn't even waste time refuting it. After all, if the guards were asleep, how did they know it was the disciples who stole the body? How could they testify to anything that happened while they were asleep?

Also, note that no attempt is made to prove that the body is still in the tomb. The empty tomb is an obvious fact no one tries to refute. Why? Because it was open and available for anyone to inspect. It couldn't be hidden or hushed up. So it had to be explained away.

Some skeptics offer the theory that the Romans or Jewish leaders took the body—but why? The last thing either of these groups would have wanted was to reinforce the Christian faith! There was no motive for them to do so. No, if anyone took the body, it would have to be the disciples. But we're back to the same problem as before: Why would the disciples willingly risk torture and death for the sake of what they knew to be a hoax?

What's more, this theory does not account for the post-Resurrection appearances of Jesus to numerous people. Another explanation is sometimes offered: that Jesus didn't really die. It is amazing that this idea is actually advanced with a straight face—but it shows how desperate the critics are to somehow circumvent the reality of the Resurrection. Imagine: Jesus, after being tortured, beaten, crucified, and run through with a spear, didn't really die, but simply passed out on the cross. Later, He revived inside the tomb and managed to wriggle loose from the yards and yards of grave linens and pounds of burial spices that were wound tightly around Him (suffocatingly, in fact!). Then, despite His weakened condition, He somehow managed to roll the stone away from the entrance of the tomb. He slipped past the Roman guards, who didn't notice the stone being moved, and escaped. It is far easier to believe in a miracle of God than in such a preposterous chain of events.

Another supposed explanation is that the Resurrection was simply a mass hallucination. Psychologists will tell you that it is impossible for hundreds of witnesses to all experience the same hallucination. Again, the skeptics are grasping at straws.

As I said earlier, it is skeptics who have the tough job. The Christian's job is easy. The evidence is not merely compelling, but overwhelming: The resurrection of Jesus Christ is an historical fact.

THE RESURRECTION MYSTERIES: ALL SOLVED!

So here again, a series of Bible mysteries has been opened, examined, and solved. Every so-called contradiction has vanished. The Resurrection is an event that took place in history, and it is forever fixed in time and space. On that glorious day of days, the most momentous event in the history of the world took place: Death was conquered. A cold, dark sky was split by a great light, and the Judaean hills burned in crimson and gold as the Lord of Glory stepped forth from the tomb—

And death forever lost its sting for those who love Him.

Jesus Christ is the One who says, "I am he that liveth, and was dead; and, behold, I am alive for evermore" (Rev. 1:18). He is the One who says, "Because I live, ye shall live also" (John 14:19). What a glorious promise He makes to us, and no skeptic has ever been able to put the slightest dent in the story of His resurrection. At a particular moment in human history, Jesus rose from the dead. He is alive today, and one day you will see Him, for the Scripture says that every eye shall see Him, and every knee shall bow before Him (Phil. 2:9–11; Rev. 1:7). One day you will greet Him as your Redeemer and Lord—or meet Him as your Judge.

Do you want to be *received* by Him—or do you want to hear those terrible words, "I never knew you: depart from me" (Matt. 7:23)? That is the most important question you will ever answer.

And there is only one rational, logical answer!

Part III

MYSTERIES OF THE CREATION, FALL, AND FLOOD

In the beginning God created the heaven and the earth.

Genesis 1:1

"There is a God in heaven, Mr. Holmes."

Sir Arthur Conan Doyle
"The Adventure of the Norwood Builder"

Mystery 8

DOESN'T THE GENESIS CREATION STORY CONTRADICT SCIENCE?

In one of Sherlock Holmes' most famous cases, "The Adventure of the Beryl Coronet," a banker comes to Holmes pleading for help. The banker has lent a large sum of money to a nobleman, taking a royal coronet (or crown) as collateral. But the crown has been stolen from the banker's locked drawer, and he is certain that his own son is the thief. Holmes thinks otherwise and proceeds to find out who among the suspects is lying and who is telling the truth. Near the end of the story, the banker pleads with Holmes to reveal the solution to the mystery.

"I will do so," Holmes replies, "and I will show you the steps by which I reached it."

Now we have before us a much deeper and more profound mystery than any that Sherlock Holmes ever solved. Yet this mystery—the mystery of the origin of the world—is one that is very easily solved. I call it "The Case of the Vanishing Evidence." The crux of the matter is this: Who is telling the truth? The book of Genesis? Or the evolutionary scientists? The solution to this case, I assure you, will leave no room for doubt. As Sherlock Holmes would say, I will reveal to you the solution to this mystery—and I will show you the steps by which the solution has been reached.

GENESIS, THE FOUNDATION

The Bible is the most influential book in the history of the world. Even skeptics will admit this truth. The Bible has been printed in more editions, translated into more languages, purchased in more volumes, and read by more people than any other book in history. Indeed, it has given birth to Western civilization.

And what is the most important book of this most important Book in history? Scientist and biblical scholar Henry Morris argues forcefully that it is Genesis. "But what about the Gospel of John, or the book of Romans?" you might ask. Yes, these are profoundly important books—yet Dr. Morris makes a very good case for the importance of Genesis when he observes that if the book of Genesis were removed from the Bible, the rest of the Bible would make no sense. The Bible without the book of Genesis would be, he says, like a building without a ground floor or a bridge without structural supports—it would collapse and become incomprehensible.

Genesis presents to us the foundational underpinnings of everything else in the Bible: the origin of the universe, the origin of order and complexity, the origin of the solar system, the origin of the atmosphere and hydrosphere, the origin of life, the origin of humanity, the origin of marriage, and the origin of evil. Genesis explains to us the origin of language, government, culture, nations, and religion. It discloses to us the origin of God's ancient chosen people, the Jews.

If Genesis were removed from the Bible, the rest of the Bible and most of life itself would become incomprehensible. In fact, as we look around at so many people who have no comprehension of the meaning of life, we see that it is precisely because they have excluded Genesis from their thinking.

THE BIBLE VERSUS SCIENCE—
OR SCIENCE VERSUS SCIENCE?

The French mathematician and astronomer, the Marquis de Laplace (1749–1827), served for several years as minister of the interior under Napoleon. During that time, he completed the first volume of his five-volume work on astronomy, *Celestial Mechanics*. He dedicated the book to Napoleon, and presented the first copy to the emperor for his approval.

After carefully reading the book, Napoleon sent for Laplace. "You have written a large book about the universe," said Napoleon. "Yet not once in these pages do you mention the Author of the universe."

"Your majesty," replied Laplace, "I have no need of that hypothesis."[1]

Many of today's scientists echo the words of Laplace: they have no need of the "God hypothesis" in explaining the origin of the universe, the earth, and human life. By contrast, the Bible begins with the words, "In the beginning *God* created the heavens and the earth" (Gen. 1:1, emphasis added). In recent years, the weight of scientific evidence has been tilting the scales in favor of the Bible and against Laplace and his atheistic brethren. Without the God hypothesis, the scientific evidence does not make sense.

In recent years, scores of books attacking the atheist orthodoxy of Darwinian evolution have been published—and these books have *not* been written by fundamentalists, evangelicals, or hard-core creationists. The authors of these books include Michael J. Behe, a biochemist at Lehigh University and author of *Darwin's Black Box: The Biochemical Challenge to Evolution* (Touchstone, 1998); English science writer Richard Milton, author of *Shattering the Myths of Darwinism* (Inner Traditions, 1997); and Michael Denton, a New Zealand-based genetics researcher and author of *Evolution: A Theory in Crisis* (Adler & Adler, 1996). These books show that the atheist pillars of evolutionary theory are collapsing.

Unfortunately, the damage has already been done. Denton, in

particular, chronicles the devastating impact that evolutionary theory has had on our world. In his book he makes this observation about the 1831 voyage of Charles Darwin aboard the HMS *Beagle*, during which Darwin made key observations that solidified his theory of evolution:

> The voyage on the *Beagle* was therefore a journey of awesome significance. Its object was to survey Patagonia; its result was to shake the foundations of western thought.

> *The Origin of Species* [which Darwin wrote following the voyage] has been referred to as "one of the most important books ever written." As far as Christianity was concerned, the advent of the theory of evolution and the elimination of traditional teleological thinking was catastrophic.[2]

Why was *The Origin of Species* called "one of the most important books ever written"? Simply because it attacked the foundation of the most important Book ever written! And what did Denton mean when he said that "the elimination of traditional teleological thinking was catastrophic"? What is teleological thinking? *Telos* is the Greek word for "purpose." It refers to the kind of purposeful thinking we all engage in every day of our lives: We believe life has a purpose and that everything we do has a plan and a design. That is what life is all about.

The Christian view has always held that human beings were created for a purpose. That purpose was summed up by the first question of the Shorter Catechism of the Westminster Confession of Faith: "What is the chief end of man?" Answer: "Man's chief end is to glorify God and to enjoy Him forever." To the evolutionist, this statement is the height of absurdity! The chief end of man? The purpose or teleology of a single human life or of the entire human race? There is none! Life, from the evolutionary point of view, has no purpose, no meaning, no significance. No wonder suicide is now the second leading cause of death among young people. When life has lost its purpose, then we must expect an epidemic of suicides, drug abuse, alcoholism, and irrational criminal behavior. That is the legacy of evolution.

Teleological thinking is anathema to the evolutionist. For the evolutionist, nothing has a purpose or an end. Those things that appear to have purposes and ends are simply the result of blind chance. Anything in nature that appears to be purposeful is merely an illusion imposed on nature by human imagination. There is no purpose in life, evolutionists tell us. Consequently, life has no significance or meaning or importance.

Stephen Jay Gould of Harvard, America's current leading evolutionist, has led the scientific charge against belief in human meaning and significance. In an article in *Scientific American*, he noted that three great scientific revolutions had served to "knock human arrogance off one pedestal after another." (He regards the belief that human beings have meaning because they are made in God's image as mere "human arrogance"!) Those three scientific revolutions are Copernicus's demonstration that the earth is not the center of the universe, Darwin's relegation of mankind to a mere branch of the animal world, and Freud's discovery of the unconscious mind, which "exploded the myth of a fully rational mind." The Darwinian revolution, however, remains unfinished, according to Gould, because people still tend to think in terms of nature's purpose, plan, and progress. Human thinking, Gould moaned, remains hopelessly teleological. He noted:

> The last pedestal of human arrogance will not be shattered until we abandon progress or complexification as a central principle and come to entertain the strong possibility that Homo sapiens [the human race] is but a tiny, late-arising twig on life's enormously arborescent bush—a small bud that would almost surely not appear

a second time if we could replant the bush from seed and let it grow again.[3]

So according to these arguments, you are not made in God's image. Your entire life is nothing more than a quirk of cosmic coincidence, and the entire human race is nothing more than an accidental little twig, without meaning or significance. There is no God and no purpose for your life.

Another consequence of Darwinism is that it has made atheism socially acceptable. You may not be aware of it, but there was a time, before Darwin, when atheists were rare. Why? Because atheism was rightly understood to be an irrational point of view. If someone said, "There is no God," the average person would look at him in amazement and say, "But look at the complexity of the universe, the design of the human body! Where did it all come from? Blind chance? You must be out of your mind!"

Atheism is as unproven and irrational today as it was before Darwin—but Darwinism has turned the tables on us all. Today if you tell someone, "I know God is real," the average person will stare at you in amazement and say, "Look at the evidence for evolution! There's no room for God in the scientific scheme of things! Creation and design? You must be out of your mind!"

Some Christians have attempted to merge the Bible and evolution into a unified worldview. Surveys show that as much as 40 percent of Americans believe that the Bible *and* evolution are true. Unfortunately, those well-intentioned but misguided people fail to recognize the absolute incompatibility between the Bible and evolution. This is nothing more than lazy thinking.

Sir Julian Huxley, the leading evolutionist in the world until his death in 1975, once said, "It is clear that the doctrine of evolution is directly antagonistic to that of Creation . . . Evolution, if consistently accepted, makes it impossible to believe the Bible."

In a debate with Christian apologist William Lane Craig, atheist

Frank Zindler, editor of *The American Atheist* magazine, made a statement that clearly draws the battle lines between evolution and Christianity:

> The most devastating thing . . . that biology did to Christianity was the discovery of biological evolution. Now that we know that Adam and Eve never were real people, the central myth of Christianity is destroyed. If there never was an Adam and Eve, there never was an original sin. If there never was an original sin, there is no need of salvation. If there is no need of salvation, there is no need of a Savior. And I submit that puts Jesus, historical or otherwise, into the ranks of the unemployed. I think that evolution is absolutely the death knell of Christianity.[4]

Well, must we accept the evolutionary view as true? Has the Genesis account been proven to be a myth? Is our existence meaningless, as so many learned minds have concluded? Who are we to argue with such scientists as Gould and Huxley? Evolution *must* be true, and that means that the Christian faith must be false, right?

But wait—we mustn't decide the case on the basis of a few pronouncements by "authorities." No, this is a mystery that should be solved on the merits of the *evidence*—not on the basis of scientific proclamation or pontification. These "authorities" would have us believe that they have arrived at their belief system purely on the basis of an objective assessment of the facts—

But have they?

EVOLUTION, PROMISCUITY, AND HOLOCAUST

Shortly before his death in 1975, Sir Julian Huxley gave a television interview that I happened to watch. Huxley was a widely respected scientist, the first director of UNESCO (United Nations Educational, Scientific, and Cultural Organization), and the world's leading evolutionist. He and his brother, novelist Aldous Huxley, were the grandsons of Thomas Henry Huxley, who was known as "Darwin's Bulldog" for his defense of Darwinian evolution. During the interview, the woman journalist asked Julian Huxley this question: "Why have so many scientists been so quick to adopt Darwin's theory of evolution?"

Huxley's answer began with these words: "The reason we scientists all jumped at *The Origin of Species* was because—"

What do you think Huxley said next? And consider this: What would the average Darwin-indoctrinated high school or college student think Huxley said next?

Your answer might be—and the student's answer almost certainly would be—"The reason we scientists all jumped at *The Origin of Species* was because Charles Darwin had amassed such overwhelming scientific evidence and such compelling, logical arguments that the conclusion was simply inescapable. The proof of Darwinism forced us, in our scientific integrity, objectivity, and honesty, to accept evolution by natural selection as a self-evident fact."

After all, that is what we are constantly told in the media, and that is what our children are taught from kindergarten on up: Evolution is a fact. The evidence is irrefutable.

But let's go back to Julian Huxley's dangling sentence. Is that, in fact, what he said? No. He didn't talk about reason and logic. He didn't talk about evidence and objectivity. Here is his answer: "The reason we scientists all jumped at *The Origin of Species* was because the idea of God interfered with our sexual mores."

In other words, Huxley and his fellow evolutionists were biased toward evolution and bigoted against Christianity *because they wanted to live sexually promiscuous lives without having to account to God.* Evolution gave them a worldview in which they could erase God from the picture, view themselves as nothing more than rutting animals, and give free rein to their sexual appetites. This is hardly an objective, evidence-based motive for adopting a scientific worldview.

Next, consider another famous British evolutionist, Sir Arthur Keith, who wrote more than twenty books defending evolution. During World War II he made this telling statement about the impact of evolution on human society: "The German Fuhrer . . . consciously sought to make the practice of Germany conform to the theory of evolution."[5] Which state was he referring to? Nazi Germany. Though Keith was a passionate supporter of evolution, he was honest enough to admit that the theory of evolution played a key role in ushering in the horrors of Nazism.

It is important to note that Darwin's earliest defender, Thomas Henry Huxley, saw various racial groups as occupying different stages in the "Great Chain of Being," with black Africans at the bottom and white European gentlemen like himself at the top. So it was a very short logical leap for Hitler's administration to go from a Darwinian belief in a "superior race" to the monstrous "final solution," the systematic extermination of six million Jews and six million other "inferior" sorts of people, including many Christians. The justification for Nazi "racial purification" policies was the Darwinian notion of evolutionary progress through the elimination of the inferior in the struggle for survival.

The title of Hitler's manifesto, *Mein Kampf* [*My Struggle*], echoed Darwin's own oft-used phrase, "the struggle for existence." In that book, Hitler propounded a number of Darwinian ideas, using many examples from the animal kingdom to underscore the survival of the fittest and the elimination of the unfit to further social progress. In a speech at the 1933 Nuremberg Nazi party rally, Hitler proclaimed that "a higher race subjects to itself a lower race . . . a right which we see in nature and which can be regarded as the sole conceivable right," a right he saw as founded in "science."[6] One of Hitler's scientific advisers, the prominent German evolutionist Ernst Haeckel, wrote that Christianity

makes no distinction of race or of color; it seeks to break down all racial barriers. In this respect the hand of Christianity is against that of Nature, for are not the races of mankind the evolutionary harvest which Nature has toiled through long ages to produce? May we not say, then, that Christianity is anti-evolutionary in its aim?[7]

Clearly, we can trace a straight line from the mind of Darwin to the minds of the Nazi exterminators. If the officials of the German government in the 1930s and 1940s had embraced the biblical view that all human beings are equally created in the image of God and are descended from Adam and Eve, it is inconceivable that the Holocaust could have ever occurred!

And Nazism isn't the only destructive ideology that evolutionary thinking has unleashed on the world. In fact, *every* major anti-Christian "ism" of the past century and a half has had its roots in evolutionary thinking:

- Karl Marx adopted the theory of evolution as the pseudoscientific foundation for his Communist ideology. He was so entranced with Darwinism, in fact, that he originally wanted to dedicate his book, Das *Kapital,* to Charles Darwin. (Darwin, largely at the urging of his wife, declined this dubious honor.)[8]

- The Italian fascist dictator Mussolini quoted evolutionary catch-phrases in many of his speeches. He believed that peace was anti-evolutionary, and that war was part of the natural struggle for survival that weeded out the weak and spurred the human race on toward new heights of progress.

- The Chinese communist leader Mao Tse-tung was also an ardent believer in Darwinism; it was out of an atheist, evolutionist mind-set that he ordered the killing of fifty-five million Chinese people.

What we believe about humanity dictates how we treat our fellow human beings. By my count, belief in the theory of evolution is directly responsible for at least 200 million deaths in the twentieth century alone. The social consequences of evolutionary thinking have been uniformly disastrous for human society. And still we continue to drum this scientific orthodoxy into the minds of one generation after another.

Why? Supposedly, because it is scientific truth. But is it true? Just what is the proof for evolution?

THE "PROOF" GOES POOF!

A textbook called *General Zoology* states, "All scientists at the present time agree that evolution is a fact." This statement reminds me of a preacher who scribbled this note in the margin of his sermon notes: "Argument weak here. Pound pulpit."

So all scientists believe in evolution, do they? Darwinism is a proven fact, is it? Again I quote the great British evolutionist, Sir Arthur Keith: "Evolution is unproved and unprovable. We believe it because the only alternative is special creation, and that is unthinkable."[9] What an astounding statement by a leading evolutionist! Whether there is evidence or not, the evolutionists cling to their theory because they simply can't stand the alternative, which is, "In the beginning God . . ."!

Is this a rational position? Is it scientific? Of course not. It is sheer, blatant, arbitrary prejudice, completely unworthy of those who call themselves men and women of science. And Sir Arthur Keith is not the only evolutionist to make this admission. Listen to some other famous scientists:

- Professor Fleischmann, zoologist from the University of Erlangen: "The Darwinian theory of descent has not a single fact to confirm it in the realm of nature. It is not the result of scientific research, but purely the product of imagination."

- The late Sir William Dawson, Canada's great geologist: "[The theory of evolution] is one of the strangest phenomena of humanity; it is utterly destitute of proof."

- Nobel prize-winning physicist Robert A. Millikan: "The pathetic thing is that we have scientists who are trying to prove evolution which no scientist can ever prove."

- Dr. Austin H. Clark, author of *The New Evolution: Zoogenesis* and one of America's greatest biologists: "So far as concerns the major groups of animals, the creationists seem to have the better of the argument. There is not the slightest evidence that any of the major groups arose from any other."

- Dr. Richard Goldschmidt—professor of zoology at the University of California and the originator of the "hopeful monster" theory of evolution—spent his entire life searching for evidence to prove evolution was true. In the end, he concluded, "Darwin's theory of natural selection has never had any proof . . . yet it has been universally accepted."

- Science journalist Roger Lewin, author of *Bones of Contention*: "The Darwinist approach has consistently been to find some supporting fossil evidence, claim it as 'proof' for 'evolution,' and then ignore all the difficulties. It is, in fact, a common fantasy, promulgated mostly by the scientific profession itself, that in the search for objective truth, data dictate conclusions. Data are just as often molded to fit preferred conclusions."

- Evolutionist science writers John Gribbin and Jeremy Cherfas write specifically of the lack of fossil evidence for human evolution in *The Monkey Puzzle*: "The publicity that accompanies every new find of fossil human remains might give the impression that by now paleontologists have a great wealth of bones to study. Not a bit of it. The known fossils of man's ancestors would all fit on a good-sized dining table, and a couple of shoeboxes would accommodate all the teeth. On this slender evidence the paleoanthropologists have built their theories."[10]

It seems that when you inspect the evidence for evolution, the "proof" goes "poof"! Darwin himself once confessed, "I have asked myself whether I may not have devoted my life to a fantasy." Tragically, he did. And so have many other evolutionists, including Julian Huxley.

Why have they committed their lives to a godless worldview based on such a thin volume of evidence? I think that many of them have chosen the fantasy of evolution over the truth of God because that is where their sinful desires and rebellion against God have led them.

AGAINST ALL ODDS

Dr. Francis Crick was the codiscoverer of DNA, and for this discovery he received the Nobel Prize. DNA is the master program of all genetic development—that double-helix molecule contains all the genetic information for making a tree, a horse, or a human being. DNA is the most complex molecule known to man. It is so fantastically complex that Crick decided to apply probability science analysis to the mystery of the origin of DNA. What are the odds, he asked, of the simplest DNA molecule arising by random chance? The god of evolution is a trinity of Matter, Chance, and Time, and evolutionists believe that, given enough time, anything is possible—even the chance formation of a complex molecule like DNA.

So Crick applied the science of probability to the question of DNA. He assumed at the outset that it would be a simple matter to prove that, given 4.5 billion years of Earth history (by the evolutionist's estimate), the chance formation of a DNA molecule was virtually inevitable. After all, evolution was a fact in his mind, so it had to have been almost a foregone conclusion. But after he calculated all the variables that had to come together by random chance in order to form the first DNA molecule, he found that the odds were practically *one chance in infinity* of that happening! According to Crick's calculations, the DNA molecule could have never evolved naturally within the entire 4.5 billion-year history of the world—and that's just one molecule. If a DNA molecule can't arise by chance in all that time, then certainly a single cell has no chance—much less an organism as complex as a human being!

Clearly, Crick had stumbled across a fatal flaw in the theory of evolution. Everything that had always been taught to schoolchildren about how life spontaneously arose in the primordial sea was a fantasy. Crick, being honest enough to accept that fact (but so steeped in his atheism that he could not accept the rational alternative, divine creation), proceeded to invent a new theory called "directed panspermia." The idea is very simple. Since life could never have arisen by natural, blind chance on earth, and since there is no God (in Crick's mind), then some advanced alien race, living on some other planet around some alien sun, must have sent spaceships out into the cosmos, scattering living cells on various planets like some intergalactic Johnny Appleseed planting apple trees across the countryside.

Now, Crick's "solution" serves only to deepen the mystery, not solve it. In logic, this is called an "infinite regress," an endless chain of reasoning that leads you only into a black hole of unknowing. To any thinking person, questions automatically arise: "Where did this advanced race of aliens come from? How did they arise? Where did their original DNA come from?"

Shortly after Crick proposed his theory, another scientist of equal reputation, astronomer Sir Fred Hoyle of Cambridge University, decided to take Crick's computations a giant step further. He examined the possibility of a single living cell arising spontaneously and by random chance—not merely within the 4.5 billion-year history of planet Earth, *but in the entire history of the universe.* Now, instead of 4.5 billion years on a single planet, we are dealing with an outside estimate of 20 billion years on any one of potentially billions of planets supposed to exist in the universe. Given all that time and all those planets, the random evolution of life somewhere in the universe should be inevitable, right?

Wrong. Hoyle calculated the probability at one chance in $10^{40,000}$—in ordinary notation, that is 1 followed by 40,000 zeros! You probably have a difficult time imagining numbers of that magnitude. Lecomte duNouy, a Nobel laureate scientist with expertise in probability science, once observed that any event that is less probable than one chance in 10^{50} will never happen. To give you an idea of the size of that number, there are about 10^{50} electrons in the entire universe. Multiply the number of electrons in the universe times ten, and you get 10^{51}. Multiply that number times ten and you get 10^{52}. You can keep multiplying times ten—10^{53}, 10^{54}, 10^{55}, 10^{56}, and eventually you see that $10^{40,000}$ is wa-a-a-ay off the scale of probability!

Conclusion: A single cell could not have evolved by chance anywhere or at any time in the entire history of the universe. It *couldn't* happen, and it *didn't* happen. So what is the explanation? The only explanation that remains is the God hypothesis. There is no third alternative.

Sir Fred Hoyle, though not an evangelical Christian, decided he had no rational choice but to embrace some form of the God hypothesis. He concluded that the only explanation for the existence of life on this planet is that life was designed by a mysterious higher order of intelligence which, for want of a better word, we may wish to call God. Hoyle endured a great deal of opposition and criticism for that statement, but he had done nothing except take his science to its logical, rational conclusion.

So the chance evolution of life is a statistical impossibility. Well, if *that* wasn't enough bad news for the evolutionists, along comes Dr. Stephen Jay Gould of Harvard—probably the leading evolutionist in America today—to make things even *worse* for his side! Along with Dr. Niles Eldredge, curator of the American Museum of Natural History, Gould made a fascinating revelation. These two leading evolutionists—both atheists and opponents of creationism—openly stated what creationists have been saying for years: There is a systematic absence of transitional forms (or so-called "missing links") in the fossil record. Darwin had predicted that there should be billions of missing links in the fossil record—we should be stumbling over fossilized transitional forms when we step out the back door. But they are simply nowhere to be found.

There is a logical conclusion that one could draw from that evidence—but Gould, an atheist, was unwilling to jump into the lap of God. He could not bring himself to be as rational as Fred Hoyle.

Instead, he decided to invent another form of evolution. He called his new idea "punctuated equilibrium."

According to this concept, species come into existence suddenly, and they remain in stasis (unchanged) for long periods of time— maybe millions and millions of years. Then, quite suddenly, many species cease to exist. Now, how are they connected to other species? Well, he said, there is a sudden burst of evolutionary activity in an isolated region where a species changes very quickly.

This concept is similar to the old "hopeful monster" idea of Dr. Richard Goldschmidt of the University of California—the idea that a lizard laid an egg and a bird, fully developed, popped out of the egg and flew away. Gould modified this view slightly, giving the bird a little more time to develop from the lizard. He imagined a relatively small population of creatures that gets separated from the rest of their species, living in a small, hostile region that creates intense "natural selection pressure," forcing the creatures to either die or adapt. These creatures mutate and evolve quickly into a noticeably new species. Then they spread and replace the parent species. How these more rapid mutations are triggered is unknown.

Now, where is the fossil evidence for punctuated equilibrium? Well, we haven't found any yet—but we're still looking! In fact, the beauty of this theory is that it claims that the lack of transitional fossils actually *proves* the theory! According to Gould, evolution took place so quickly that it didn't leave a trace! Thus, no evidence equals proof!

It is a most amazing inversion of logic—and a tribute to Gould's ability to weave a seemingly plausible tale out of a sheer vacuum of evidence. This concept is also a tribute to Stephen Jay Gould's public relations skills, since he was able to take a discredited theory ("hopeful monsters") and dress it up with a new name ("punctuated equilibrium") and sell it as a new idea—a brilliant example of a "Madison Avenue Makeover"!

But the greatest irony of the entire "punctuated equilibrium" story is how cleverly Gould has reshaped evidence *against* evolution into evidence *for* evolution. If you go back to the beginning of the Darwinian controversy, before the turn of the century, you discover that geologist Adam Sedgwick (a good friend of Darwin's but an ardent opponent of his theory) used the same arguments that Gould uses today—*but he used them as evidence for creation, not evolution.* Sedgwick was considered one of the greatest geologists who ever lived, yet he was convinced by the findings of his own geological work that species appeared suddenly, abruptly, without transitional forms. Those species remained in stasis for long periods of times, then disappeared—all in perfect accordance with the creationist worldview.

Some would say that the doctrine of creation is not really that important to the Bible as a whole. I strongly disagree. The first phrase in the first sentence of Genesis makes this all-important statement: "In the beginning God created the heavens and the earth." That is where the Bible begins, and that is where all of life and theology and action ultimately has its beginning.

Our beliefs shape our actions. What we believe about the origin of the universe and the origin of life affects how we live. You cannot build a moral system on an evolutionary foundation. In a world where Darwinism reigns, objective morality collapses—and with it, society as a whole.

This terrible truth was evident to Darwin's spiritually discerning and wise friend, Adam Sedgwick. On November 24, 1859, immediately after reading *The Origin of Species* for the first time, Sedgwick took pen in hand and wrote these grim words to his friend, Charles Darwin:

> We are point blank at issue—There is a moral or metaphysical part of
> nature as well as a physical. A man who denies this is deep in the mire
> of folly. Tis the crown & glory of organic science that it does thro' final
> cause, link material to moral. You have ignored this link; &, if I do not
> mistake your meaning, you have done your best . . . to break it. Were
> it possible (which thank God it is not) to break it, humanity in my

mind, would suffer a damage that might brutalize it—& sink the human race into a lower grade of degradation than any into which it has fallen since its written records tell us of its history.[11]

Sedgwick was wrong when he said that it is not possible to break the link between material and moral. That link has been broken, and we are witnessing today the fulfillment of Sedgwick's dire prophecy: the human race is sinking into degradation. People, believing themselves to be nothing more than soulless animals, have created a hell on earth of promiscuity, perversion, abortion on demand, alcohol and drug abuse, pornography, child abuse, domestic violence, street violence, schoolyard violence, and more. When people *think* they are nothing but animals, they *behave* as nothing but animals. If there is no Creator, there are no absolutes, no morality, no truth.

Ken Ham, executive director of the creationist organization Answers in Genesis (www.answersingenesis.org), told me of a student—a devout evolutionist—who came to him and asked, "Why should I follow the rules of society or religion? Why can't I write my own rules about life and make up my own moral code?"

"Oh," said Ken, "you want to write your own rules and make up your own morality as you go along."

"That's right."

"Fine—but just remember that if everyone gets to make up his own rules, then it's okay for me to shoot you."

"What?" the student responded, taken aback. "That's not okay at all!"

"Why not?"

"It's not right."

"Why isn't it right?" asked Ken. "Who says it's not right?"

"Well, everybody knows it's wrong to kill people."

"Why?" Ken probed. "As long as every person gets to make up his own rules, then no one can say what I choose to do is wrong."

"Well," the student pondered uncertainly, "that sounds fair, but . . ."

"Of course, it's fair. Now here's my first rule. People like you are dangerous and must be eliminated from society."

At this point the student was beginning to get the idea. A society *must* have objective standards of morality, or it breaks down. When there are no objective rules, no moral standards, no agreed-upon mores, we have chaos in our streets, our classrooms, our families, our government, our society. The foundation of our society is morality, and morality descends from God. Once you eliminate God, you eliminate morality—and the foundations of society crumble. As the psalmist wrote, "If the foundations be destroyed, what can the righteous do?" (Ps. 11:3).

The foundations of our society have been crumbling, even while the scientific foundations of the theory of evolution are crumbling. Yet the foundations of our faith remain as firm as ever. The evidence that scientists have sought to prop up Darwinism has never materialized, even as the evidence for the destructive nature of Darwin's ideas continues to mount. Like the boy in the story "Jack and the Beanstalk," we are laying the axe to the base of the beanstalk. The beanstalk of evolution may tower over our society today, but I fully believe we are going to see the day (and I hope I live to see it) when the giant comes crashing to earth and the land is restored to a solid foundation for life, ethics, faith, and—yes—science.

So this mystery is solved. Does the Genesis account of creation contradict science? Yes—and no. Yes, Genesis contradicts the statements of many atheist scientists. But no, Genesis does not contradict *true science*. For the most scientifically accurate statement that has ever been written about origins is this:

"In the beginning God created the heavens and the earth."

DOESN'T THE BOOK OF GENESIS CONTRADICT ITSELF?

Wilson Mizner was a popular writer of the 1930s. He lived in New York, and was equally at ease hobnobbing with financiers and long-shoremen, with the literary elite and heavyweight boxers. For a while, he even managed a boxer named Stanley Ketchel, also known as the Michigan Assassin. One day, over breakfast in his apartment, Mizner explained the theory of evolution to Ketchel. Though the boxer was not exactly a Rhodes scholar, he was thoroughly fascinated by the idea of one species changing into another.

After breakfast, Ketchel sat down in a chair by the window, lost in contemplation. Mizner left the apartment, did some errands, lunched with friends, then returned to the apartment. Ketchel was still in the same chair, lost in thought. Mizner invited the boxer to join him and some friends for dinner and a night on the town. "No thanks," said Ketchel. "I'll just stay here." Mizner shrugged and left. Hours later, past midnight, Mizner turned the key of his apartment door, stepped inside—

And there was the Michigan Assassin, in the very same chair, still lost in contemplation. It seemed he had not moved from that spot all day long. "Ketchel," said Mizner, "how long are you going to sit there?"

Without warning, Ketchel jumped to his feet, snarling with rage.

"That evolution stuff you told me this mornin' was nuthin' but bunk!" he shouted. Then he pointed to the goldfish bowl that Mizner kept in the window beside the chair. "I been watchin' them fish all day long and they haven't changed one bit!"

Clearly, the Michigan Assassin had failed to grasp the finer points of the theory of evolution! And yet, many highly educated, highly intelligent proponents of evolution and atheism make just as foolish a mistake in their approach to the creation story in Genesis.

The shelves of your local Borders or Barnes & Noble groan under the weight of books that claim to debunk the Bible—books with such titles as *Self-Contradictions of the Bible*, *The Atheist Debater's Handbook*, *The Case Against God*, *The Skeptic's Guide to the Bible*, *The Encyclopedia of Biblical Errancy*, and *Fables & Mythology of the Bible*. Internet Web sites abound, operated by self-professed "infidels" and "freethinkers" who delight in playing a game of "gotcha!" with the Bible. As soon as they identify a supposed contradiction in the Bible, they shout, "Gotcha! Here's a Bible blunder! So much for the Christian faith!"

All of the atheists' claims of biblical contradictions make as much sense as sitting in front of a bowlful of goldfish, waiting for evolution to take place. Seeming contradictions in the Bible are almost always the result of careless interpretation of the Scriptures on the part of the hostile critics. This is particularly true of one of the critics' favorite "contradictions," the alleged discrepancy between the creation accounts in Genesis 1 and Genesis 2.

And that is the next Bible mystery we will explore.

GENESIS 1 AND GENESIS 2: NO CONTRADICTION

Genesis 1 tells us that the heavens and the earth were created in six days. The creatures of the sea, air, and land were created on the fifth and sixth days, after which God created the first human beings. But, say the critics, Genesis 2:19 shows the animals being created *after* Adam and Eve. This, they claim, is a case of the Bible contradicting itself.

But is it? Here is what Genesis 2:19 says:

And out of the ground the LORD God formed every beast of the field, and every fowl of the air; and brought them unto Adam to see what he would call them: and whatsoever Adam called every living creature, that was the name thereof.

A superficial glance tells us that this verse suggests that Adam was formed first, then the animals, and then (2:21–25) God created Eve. If this was actually what Genesis 2:19 said, then there would clearly be a contradiction between Genesis 1 and Genesis 2.

Let me ask you this: Is it reasonable to suppose that the writer of Genesis and the later Jewish scholars who interpreted these passages were so stupid that they could not spot such an obvious "discrepancy"? Did we really have to wait several thousand years for the skeptics and atheists to come along and point out this glaring "error"?

The fact is that Hebrew scholars have studied this passage for centuries and never saw any conflict between Genesis 1 and Genesis 2. Why? *Because there is no conflict.* The Hebrew language does not contain the precise verb tense forms that English has; in Hebrew, you can only understand the verb tense that is intended by paying attention to the context. Since it is obvious from Genesis 1 that the beasts and birds were created before Adam, Hebrew scholars understood the actual meaning of 2:19 to be (note the italicized words):

Now the LORD God *had formed* out of the ground all the beasts of the field and all the birds of the air. He brought them to the man to see what he would name them; and whatever the man called each living creature, that was its name.

This is how Jewish scholars have always understood this verse. This verse does not offer a second and contradictory creation account. It simply recalls a fact previously recorded in Genesis 1—that God had *already* formed the beasts and birds, and *now* He brought them to Adam to be named. Once you see this verse in its cultural and narrative context, the so-called contradiction evaporates.

One of the reasons critics see a contradiction where none exists is that they falsely view Genesis 1 and Genesis 2 as two different and opposing creation accounts—a view that was superimposed onto Genesis by liberal textual critics of the nineteenth century. A careful and unbiased reading of the first two chapters of Genesis shows that this is a single, flowing narrative. Genesis 2 doesn't present a different creation account from chapter 1—this is obvious from the fact that Genesis 2 makes no attempt to explain the creation of the heavens and the earth, the atmosphere, the oceans and land, the sun, moon, stars, and so forth. Genesis 2 deals specifically with the creation of Adam and Eve and the happy phase of their unfallen condition in the Garden of Eden.

Genesis 1 is the creation story from the perspective of the Creator. It is a wide-screen view. Genesis 2 is the creation story from the human perspective. It is a close-up view. It is more intimate. Whereas Genesis 1 is the landscape view, Genesis 2 is the portrait view.

The critics look at the chapter divisions in our English Bible—chapter divisions that did not exist throughout most of the centuries that Genesis has existed—and they see a division between the "two creation stories" of chapters 1 and 2. But that is not how the writer of Genesis divided this book. The writer of Genesis considered 1:1 to 2:4 to be a single, consistent narrative that he called "the genealogy of the heavens and the earth."

At Genesis 5:1 (NKJV) we encounter the word *genealogy* (*toledoth*) again:

> This is the book of the genealogy of Adam. In the day that God created man, He made him in the likeness of God.

This statement marks the end of the second section of the book, Genesis 2:5 to 5:1. It also shows that the second section had a specific purpose—to tell about the origin of Adam. Here is yet more proof that this passage was not intended to be a "second creation story," as the critics charge.

Significantly, this word *toledoth* or *genealogy* appears in ten key places in Genesis, marking off ten key sections of the book:

Genesis 1:1–2:4	The origin of the heavens and the earth
Genesis 2:5–5:1	The origin of Adam and Eve
Genesis 5:2–6:9	The origin of Noah
Genesis 6:10–10:1	The origin of the sons of Noah
Genesis 10:2–11:10	The origin of Shem
Genesis 11:11–11:27	The origin of the family of Abraham
Genesis 11:28–25:12	The origin of the family of Ishmael
Genesis 25:13–25:19	The origin of the family of Isaac
Genesis 25:20–36:1	The origin of the family of Esau
Genesis 36:2–37:2	The origin of the family of Jacob

Genesis 5:1 clearly tells us that the focus of Genesis 2:5 to 5:1 is Adam, not the creation of the heavens and the earth. The writer of Genesis has already informed us that the creation of the universe was already told in full in Genesis 1:1 to 2:4. To the Hebrew reader, Genesis 2:19 says, in effect, "As you recall from chapter 1, God had already formed the beasts and birds. Then He created Adam and He brought the beasts and birds He had made earlier and He presented them to Adam to be named."

The book of Genesis cannot be read like a modern American novel in which the narrative starts at the beginning, proceeds to the middle, and ends at the end. Genesis is an ancient document written in a mode that was common in Middle Eastern cultures, and it develops its narrative in a way we are not accustomed to in our culture. Like many historical accounts of that era, it begins with a chronological overview of events, followed by a more detailed and dramatic close-up view. Accordingly, Genesis 1:1 to 2:4 deals with the chronology of creation;

from 2:5 on, Genesis deals with the stories of individual people. When we approach the text with a mind-set of cross-cultural understanding instead of antireligious hostility, the meaning of the text becomes plain, and the mystery disappears.

WHERE DID CAIN GET HIS WIFE?

As this book was being written, I happened to see a televised interview with a woman scientist. In this interview, she reflected on an experience she had as a six-year-old girl in Sunday school. During class, her teacher had asked if any of the children had a question to ask. So the little girl raised her hand and asked, "Where did Mrs. Cain come from?" In other words, where did Cain get his wife?

The Sunday school teacher could not answer the question. In fact, this question caused such a stir that the Sunday school superintendent sent home a letter to the girl's parents informing them that their daughter was no longer welcome in the Sunday school.

I was grieved to hear that story. That little girl grew up thinking that her silly little question was so profound that it had stumped the entire Sunday school and had sent Christians fleeing in fear. As a result, she had grown up to become a smug atheist who considered the Bible to be nothing but a book of fairy tales.

To this day, that question—where did Cain get his wife?—is a favorite Bible-Thumper Stumper among critics and skeptics of the Bible. Tragically, many Christians are terrified of this question. Yet this seeming Bible "mystery" can actually be solved quite simply.

According to the Bible, all human beings are descendants of Adam and Eve. It was necessary, therefore, that there be intermarriage between close relatives, including brother and sister, in the earliest generations of the human race. In those days, of course, the entire human race belonged to a single family, so the choice of marriage prospects was limited, to say the least. Today, of course, we would consider such relationships incestuous and forbidden. God did, in fact, prohibit incest in

Leviticus as a way of preventing the kinds of harmful birth deformities caused by inbreeding.

In the days of Adam, however, such deformities were not an issue and could not have occurred, because these deformities are the result of genetic mutations that need time to accrue within a population. So as distasteful as the idea might be to our modern sensibilities, the act of intermarriage within one family would not have presented a moral, medical, or genetic problem in the time of Adam. Those first few generations would have passed down undamaged genes.

Creation scientists believe that the Flood of Noah caused changes in the atmosphere that resulted in more harmful radiation passing through the atmosphere and causing genetic damage and mutations. The increase in radiation probably accelerated the degeneration of the human body, reducing human life span and increasing the probability of deformities when blood relatives married. In time, it became necessary for Moses to give mankind the laws against incest (Lev. 18–20), which stand to this day.

Now, does this mean that Cain married his sister? Not necessarily. Genesis 5:4 tells us, "And the days of Adam after he had begotten Seth were eight hundred years: *and he begat sons and daughters*" (emphasis added). How many sons and daughters? The Bible doesn't say, but over a span of almost a millennium, the number of Adam's children could have easily been quite great—perhaps scores or even hundreds of children. Given that amount of time, Cain might have married his sister or even a cousin. The important thing to remember is that Cain's marriage took place centuries before God outlawed incest in the book of Leviticus. In Cain's day, such marriages were perfectly lawful.

The question of where Cain got his wife raises an important principle in regard to solving Bible mysteries: *Never allow an unbeliever to frame the question.* Very often unbelievers try to stump Christians by framing a question based on a false premise. For example, skeptics and atheists often try to stump Christians by framing the question this way: "The Bible says that Cain went to the land of Nod, east of Eden, and there he found a wife. But how could that be, if Adam, Eve, Cain, and Seth were the only people on earth?"

Have you spotted the false premise in this question? Let's look at the Bible and see if it really says what the skeptics claim it says.

> And Cain went out from the presence of the LORD, and dwelt in the land of Nod, on the east of Eden. And Cain knew his wife; and she conceived, and bare Enoch: and he builded a city, and called the name of the city, after the name of his son, Enoch. (Gen. 4:16–17)

Critics claim that this passage says that Cain found his wife in the land of Nod—yet, the passage does not say that! Clearly, what this passage indicates is that Cain went to the land of Nod and took his wife with him! And where did he get his wife? From among the many daughters of Adam, of course. So this should be a lesson to us all: Never accept a skeptic's interpretation of Scripture. Never accept the skeptic's framing of the question. Always read the passage for yourself to see what God's Word really says.

And remember: Most Bible mysteries are easily solved by those who are open to God's Word rather than hostile to it.

A BOATLOAD OF QUESTIONS

Peter Sparrow, of the creationist organization Answers in Genesis, tells of one skeptic he met in a shopping mall. "How can you believe that stuff about the Flood and the ark?" the young man asked. "There's no way Moses could get all those animals in the ark!"

"Well, maybe Moses couldn't have," Sparrow replied, "but then, it wasn't Moses who built the ark—it was Noah." Sparrow proceeded to question the young man to find out how he could be so certain of his facts. "How many animals would Noah have had to fit aboard the ark?" he asked.

The young man shrugged.

123

"Well, how big was the ark?" asked Sparrow.

Again, the young man didn't know.

"So what you're telling me is that an undetermined number of animals couldn't possibly fit into an ark of unknown size?"

"Well, how does anyone know how big the ark was?"

"The exact dimensions are given right in the Bible," said Sparrow.

"Oh," the man said, frowning. "But how can anyone know how many animals Noah had to take on the ark?"

"Simple. You go to any book on taxonomy—"

"What's that?"

"Animal classification. It's really a very simple matter to figure out how many land animals and birds had to fit on the ark, including the extinct varieties."

And Peter Sparrow proceeded to explain to the man that the story of Noah's ark is perfectly reasonable—once you know all the facts. Like so many people these days, this unfortunate skeptic based his unbelief on his own ignorance.[1] The story of Noah's ark is another Genesis account that critics often seize upon to "prove" that the Bible is nothing but a pack of contradictions, lies, and myths. But here again, the Bible proves itself steadfast and reliable.

Creation scientists have conducted a careful analysis of the ark's capacity and storage requirements, and here is what they have found: Genesis 6:15 tells us that the ark measured 300 by 50 by 30 cubits. We know that there were two measurements called cubits in antiquity: One was 18 inches in length, and the other was 24 inches in length. But to be on the conservative side, let's use the smaller cubit. That would make the dimensions of the ark roughly 450 feet long (that's a football field and a half in length!) by 75 feet wide by 45 feet high. Its capacity, therefore, was *more than 1.5 million cubic feet*. To put this in visual terms, the ark's capacity was the equivalent of 522 railroad stock cars, each with a capacity of 240 sheep.

Furthermore, the ark wasn't a ship. There is a reason it is called an ark and not a ship or a boat—Noah's ark was not a sailing vessel. It had no sail, no oars, no rudder, no means of propulsion whatsoever. It was just a big floating box. Noah never sailed it anywhere. It was designed for sheer capacity. So every one of those 1.5 million cubic feet was sheer storage space.

I think it is important to note that God instructed Noah to make the ark with only a single door (Gen. 6:16). When God's judgment came upon all the earth, there was only one place to hide, and only one door through which to pass into safety. That principle still holds true today. We know that God's judgment will one day be poured out upon the earth again—not with a flood this time (God promised never to flood the earth again), but with fire. When God's final judgment comes against mankind, there will still be just one door into the ark. Christ is our Ark of Safety in the time of judgment, and our only hope for safety is to pass through that narrow door and place our trust in Him. That is the message of Noah's ark to us today.

Some people today don't believe there ever was a Flood. But if that is so, if there never was a Great Flood, then why is the story of a world-wide flood so indelibly impressed upon the memory of mankind all around the world? There is no more universal story in world folklore than the story of the Great Flood. It is told in the most ancient documents of Babylonia, Egypt, Greece, India, China, Polynesia, Native America, and many other cultures. Having been handed down and preserved in various oral and written traditions, the story is told with varying degrees of distortion—but the outline of the story is always the same. The vessel is not necessarily an ark; it may be a boat, a canoe, or a raft; it may house eight people or six or two or twelve. But the basic story is always there: God was displeased with mankind because of their sin, and He destroyed the world with a Great Flood. Could such a universal belief have sprung up in culture after culture without any basis in historical fact? That would be inconceivable.

A final note on the story of Noah: Some Bible critics claim to find a discrepancy between Genesis 6:19, where God tells Noah to take two of every species onto the ark, and Genesis 7:2–3, where God tells Noah to take seven pairs of animals onto the ark. Here again, critics base their judgment on a cursory glance at Scripture instead of actually reading what it says. In Genesis 6:19, God gives Noah a general command to take one pair of all animals aboard the ark. Then, in chapter 7, verses 2–3, God refines that commandment by saying:

> Of every clean beast thou shalt take to thee by sevens, the male and his female: and of beasts that are not clean by two, the male and his female. Of fowls also of the air by sevens, the male and the female; to keep seed alive upon the face of all the earth.

Here God makes a clear distinction between animals that were considered ritually clean—that is, animals that are fit to be sacrificed to God—and those that are ordinary, nonsacrificial animals. We see the importance of this command in Genesis 8:20, where Noah comes out of the ark following the Flood and builds an altar to the Lord and sacrifices several of the clean animals and birds as a burnt offering to God. Had he not taken extra pairs of the clean animals aboard the ark, he could not have made a sacrifice to God without causing the extinction of several prime species!

So another Bible mystery is solved. The book of Genesis easily survives the most vicious attacks of the critics. Alleged inconsistencies and contradictions melt away in the glare of reasonable analysis of the biblical evidence. As we shall see throughout our probe of Bible mysteries, the Christian faith is a reasonable faith, supported by proof upon proof upon proof. What seems a mystery at first becomes obvious once you see it in the right light.

We have considered the events "in the beginning," and they point to one conclusion: God's Word stands firm, it is reliable, it is unshakable.

But the game is still afoot! Come, my friend! On to the *next* mystery!

Part IV

MYSTERIES OF THE NATURE OF GOD

Canst thou by searching find out God? canst thou find out the Almighty unto perfection?

Job 11:7

The facts slowly evolve before your own eyes, and the mystery clears gradually away as each new discovery furnishes a step which leads on to the complete truth.

Sir Arthur Conan Doyle
"The Adventure of the Engineer's Thumb"

THE MYSTERY OF THE INCARNATION: IS JESUS GOD OR THE SON OF GOD?

Who is Jesus Christ to you? Would you be willing to die for the sake of this Man named Jesus?

Let me tell you about someone who was faithful to Jesus to the very point of death—death by torture, death by fire. His name was Polycarp, and he was an early church father. Historical tradition records that the apostle John himself mentored and discipled Polycarp before Polycarp became Bishop of Smyrna, a city on the west coast of Turkey. If the name Smyrna sounds familiar, it's because it was one of the seven churches of Asia listed at the beginning of Revelation, and it was identified as a church that endured intense persecution.

As an old man, Polycarp was arrested and tried for the "crime" of being a Christian. His life stands as a challenge to you and me: If we were arrested for such a crime, would there be enough evidence to convict us? Clearly, Polycarp's life left evidence aplenty that he was a devout and committed follower of Christ. He was guilty as charged.

Even so, Polycarp could have easily saved himself from torture and death. The magistrate was reluctant to send this gentle old man to his death, and he pleaded with Polycarp to accept a deal: All Polycarp had to do to save his life was curse Christ and swear by the luck of Caesar—

just say a few words, and he would be free to live out the rest of his life in peace. But Polycarp refused to utter those words.

"Eighty-six years I have served Jesus," said the old bishop, "and He never did me any wrong. How can I blaspheme my King, who has saved me?"

So the magistrate reluctantly sentenced Polycarp to be burned at the stake. He was bound to the stake by iron bands, and the wood was piled up around him. As he waited for the pyre to be torched, Polycarp prayed aloud, "Lord God Almighty, I bless You that You have thought me worthy of this day and hour, to be numbered among the martyrs, to share in the cup of Christ, for resurrection to eternal life, for soul and body in the incorruptibility of the Holy Spirit. May I be received today as a rich and acceptable sacrifice."

The flames rose about him, yet he did not plead for mercy or even cry out in pain. He simply continued praying, thanking God for the honor of dying a martyr's death for the sake of Jesus Christ. Finally, the magistrate could not bear to watch Polycarp's suffering, so he ordered a soldier to kill the old man with a dagger through the heart.

Who was this Man named Jesus, for whom Polycarp would go willingly, even joyfully, to a martyr's death? Polycarp was hardly alone. Millions of people have withstood torture and gone to an early death for the sake of the Lord Jesus Christ. They believed in this Man who said, "I am the resurrection and the life" (John 11:25). Some went to the Coliseum to be fed to lions for the amusement and entertainment of the decadent Roman masses. Some were covered with pitch, mounted on poles, and set ablaze—living human torches to light Nero's gardens. Some were put in sacks with deadly serpents and other beasts. They were tortured and killed in every hideous way the depraved mind of man could invent. But whenever ten were killed, another twenty rose up to take their place. They went to their deaths singing hymns of praise to the One who died for their sins.

Who is this Man named Jesus? If He were just a man like any other man, even if He were merely a great moral teacher, as so many claim, then Polycarp and all his fellow martyrs went needlessly to their horrible deaths. They suffered torture and lost their lives for nothing. If He were just a man, then His followers and martyrs are nothing but poor, pitiful, deluded fools.

But I submit to you that they didn't die for nothing, because Jesus Christ is much more than a mere man. He is the Word made flesh—God in human form. And that makes all the difference. Down through the ages of history, all true churches have held that Jesus Christ is God. The surest sign that a "church" is actually a cult is if it denies the divinity of Christ.

THE CENTERPIECE OF HISTORY

A lady once said to me, "We really shouldn't talk about Jesus being God, because when He was on earth, God was in Heaven, don't you know."

As a matter of fact, I did know that. God, of course, is in Heaven, He is within us as Christians, He is around us, He is everywhere at once, He is omnipresent. But why should the fact that God is in Heaven suggest that Jesus is not God? Our God, after all, is a triune God—three Persons in one Godhead. The doctrine of the Trinity is the foundation of all Christian doctrine. If we accept the fact of the Trinity, then we have no problem accepting the fact that Jesus is God the Son, one of the three Persons of the Trinity.

This is not a minor theological point—this is a core issue of the Christian faith. In John 20:31, the apostle John tells us that his Gospel was written "that ye might believe that Jesus is the Christ, the Son of God; and that believing ye might have life through his name." Here is a clear statement of Jesus' identity: He is the Son of God.

But let's backtrack just three verses and read what Thomas—the disciple known as Doubting Thomas—said when he encountered the risen Christ: "My Lord and my God!" (John 20:28) That is just one of many places in Scripture that make it clear that Jesus is God. In Matthew 1:23, the writer quotes Isaiah 7:14, which says that the name of the virgin-born Child-Messiah shall be called Immanuel, "which is translated, 'God with us,'" or God in human form. The first verse of John's Gospel makes it equally clear:

> In the beginning was the Word [that is, Jesus], and the Word was with God, *and the Word was God* . . . All things were made by him; and without him was not any thing made that was made . . . And the Word was made flesh, and dwelt among us." (John 1:1, 3, 14, emphasis added)

In Titus 2:13, Paul calls Him "our great God and Savior Jesus Christ." In 1 John 5:20, the evangelist calls Jesus "the true God and eternal life." And in one of the great Old Testament prophecies of the Messiah, Isaiah 9:6, we read: "And his name shall be called Wonderful, Counsellor, The mighty God, The everlasting Father, The Prince of Peace." There are other Bible passages I could cite, but the scriptural case has been clearly made, and there is no ambiguity whatsoever.

Jesus is *God* and He is *the Son of God*. Some critics object, "But that's a contradiction! How can one person be both God and God's Son? That makes no sense!" But it does make sense. It makes sense in the same way that God the Father is also God; and it makes sense in the same way that the Holy Spirit is also God. Jesus is God in that He is God the Son.

Do you truly believe that? Is the absolute Godhood of Jesus a reality in your life right now? Or does your faith run aground on this point? Who do you say Jesus is? Do you see Him as fully God—or merely human?

A great German writer, Johann Wolfgang von Goethe (1749–1832), once observed, "The conflict of faith and unbelief remains the proper, the only, the deepest theme of the history of the world." What was true in Goethe's day is no less true today: The great drama that is unfolding before us is the drama of the conflict between faith and unbelief. When that drama has been consummated, when the last actor exits the stage, there will only be one Person standing, clothed in white robes, occupying the spotlight at center stage. That Person is Jesus Christ.

This world tries to ignore Him. The corrupt systems of this world try to erase all knowledge and memory of Him from our schools, our media, our government, our public occasions and celebrations. Yet millions of times a day, whenever a check is dated or a date is published on a newspaper masthead, the world acknowledges that it has been X number of years since the birth of the Savior. Knowingly or unknowingly, millions of people bear witness every day to the birth of the greatest Person who ever lived. He is the centerpiece of human history. All human events are reckoned according to where they fall relative to this one solitary life—whether Before Christ or Anno Domini. Every time atheists and agnostics date a check or celebrate the New Year, they are forced to bear testimony to the importance of Jesus Christ.

LIAR, LUNATIC—OR LORD?

It has been roughly two thousand years since a little Jewish baby was placed in a manger in the little Judaean village of Bethlehem—yet that manger contained something greater than the entire universe. It contained God the Son. And on Him the Church stands. The study of the question "Who is Jesus?" is the core question of the existence of the Church. It's the central question of history, of our individual souls, and our eternal future.

Jesus once put this very question to His disciples, asking them, "Whom do men say that I the Son of man am?" (Matt. 16:13). They answered that some thought he was John the Baptist, or the reincarnation of Elijah or Jeremiah or some other Old Testament prophet. Then He asked them (v. 15), "But whom say ye that I am?" And that is when Peter made his famous confession of faith, "Thou art the Christ, the Son of the living God" (v. 16). Jesus is still asking us today, "Who do you say I am?"

George Gallup put that same question to a cross-section of the American people in a Gallup Poll entitled "How America Sees Jesus." The poll revealed:

133

- 81 percent of Americans profess to be Christians (versus 5 percent atheists, 2 percent Jews, and various assorted other beliefs).

- Roughly 80 percent of Americans believe Jesus is the Son of God.

- *Only 42 percent* believe that Jesus is God!

Now, that is a tremendous discrepancy! Only about half of those who believe Jesus is the Son of God believe He is God.

No doubt some of the confusion in the minds of these Americans is due to the error that is sold as entertainment in our culture. For example, in the Carl Reiner movie *Oh, God!* (1977), John Denver plays a man who talks directly to God, played by George Burns. At one point in that irreverent film, John Denver asks, "Was Jesus the Son of God?" The cigar-chomping "God" replies, "Jesus was my son. Buddha was my son. The man who said, 'There's no room at the inn'—he was my son, too. Let's move on." In other words, Jesus was *a* son of God among many, but certainly not *the* Son of God, and not God in human flesh.

Over the years, I've asked many people, "Who is Jesus?" The answers I get are always fascinating. Frankly, many people are confused. "Well, I'm not sure, really," they often say. "I guess I can go along with the idea that He is the Son of God—but I don't buy the idea that He was God Himself." At that point, I will sometimes probe a little further to see if they are really thinking about what they are saying or just parroting some cliché they have heard. "Well," I say, "I am a son of God. Is Jesus any different from me?" Occasionally I have received a truly shocking reply: "No, not that I can see." I assure you, anyone who does not think Christ is different from me knows little about either of us!

As Christians, you and I are children of God—but when Jesus called Himself the Son of God, He meant something very different from that. In many places in the Gospels, He called Himself "the Son of man," which is a messianic title taken from the Old Testament book of Daniel. Rarely in the Gospels does He make the simple declarative statement, "I am the Son of God," but in many places He speaks of God as His Father, and when others call Him the Son of God, He receives that title and affirms that it is the truth. For example, when he stood before the chief priests of the Sanhedrin, shortly before being handed over to Pilate to be crucified, they asked Him, "Art thou then the Son of God?" And He answered, "Ye [rightly] say that I am." At this, the chief priests flew into a rage! "What need we any further witness? For we ourselves have heard of his own mouth" (Luke 22:70–71).

John 10 records another confrontation between Jesus and the Jewish leaders. In verse 30, He states, "I and my Father are one." Clearly, He is making a shocking claim—the claim that He is one with God! At this, the Jewish leaders took up stones in their hands and were ready to stone Him to death for the sin of blasphemy—"because that thou, being a man, makest thyself God" (v. 33). The Jews understood quite clearly what He was saying. He was claiming, in no uncertain terms, to be almighty God. This claim was validated by His life, death, and resurrection.

Remember, the Bible repeatedly warns that we are to worship God alone, and that no mere created being is ever to be worshipped. This is what John discovered at the end of the book of Revelation:

> And when I had heard and seen, I fell down to worship before the feet of the angel which shewed me these things. Then saith he unto me, See thou do it not: for I am thy fellowservant, and of thy brethren the prophets, and of them which keep the sayings of this book: *worship God*. (Rev. 22:8–9, emphasis added)

Worship God and *only* God! To worship any mere creature is idolatry and blasphemy. Yet, throughout the Gospels, again and again, we find that Jesus received and even blessed the worship of men. On Palm Sunday, when He made His triumphal entry into Jerusalem, throngs of people praised and worshipped Him; when the Pharisees rebuked Him for receiving their worship, He replied that if the people kept silent, "the stones would immediately cry out" to worship Him (Luke 19:40). He was also worshipped by the Magi; He was worshipped by the leper; He was worshipped by the disciples; He was worshipped by the women and the disciples after the Resurrection. He was worshipped over and over again, culminating in that great statement of worship, wrenched from the amazed lips of Thomas: "My Lord and my God!"

I once had a conversation with a gentleman who thought that Jesus was just a man like anyone else. I said, "I think I have some astonishing good news for you. According to the Bible and the historic Christian faith, Jesus of Nazareth not only *was* but *is* the infinite, eternal Creator of the universe—the almighty God." His reaction was profound. Instantly, his eyes filled with tears. "I have never heard that before," he said, "and yet I have always thought that is the way it ought to be, if Jesus is who He seems to be." My friend, that is precisely the way it is! Jesus Christ is God. If He were not God, He would be a mere created being. The Trinity does not consist of the Father, the Holy Spirit, and a created being called the Son. The Son of God is fully God.

The fact that Jesus Christ is God incarnate—God in human flesh—is the most basic, most important, most distinctive teaching of the Christian faith. Only Jesus claimed to be divine, and only Christianity claims its Founder is divine. Moses made no such claim, nor did Buddha, nor did Muhammad, nor did Lao-tse, nor did Confucius, nor did any other religious teacher. Only Jesus made that claim—and it is the sheer audacity of His claim that created such chaos and indignation among the Jewish leaders. C. S. Lewis, in *Mere Christianity*, describes the shock waves that Jesus created with His claim to be God in human form:

> Among these Jews there suddenly turns up a man who goes about talking as if He was God. He claims to forgive sins. He says He has always existed. He says He is coming to judge the world at the end of time . . . What this man said was, quite simply, the most shocking thing that has ever been uttered by human lips.[1]

Many people today say that Jesus was a "good man"—but such faint praise is, in fact, a lie! To call Him a "good man" may sound like you are speaking well of Christ, but, in fact, you are libeling Him, for it is nothing more than a mealy-mouthed denial of His Godhood. Jesus Himself had to deal with the same patronizing nonsense two thousand years ago. In Luke 18, a leader of the people came to Jesus and said, "Good Master, what shall I do to inherit eternal life?" (v. 18) Jesus replied, in effect, "Hold it right there! Why do you call Me good? There is only One who is good—God Himself."

Now, just a few verses earlier, Jesus had been teaching that all men are sinful—and now this man was calling Him good. So Jesus impaled the rich young ruler on the horns of a dilemma: If Jesus is merely a man, then He is not good, for all men are sinful! But if Jesus is good, then He is God, because there is only One who is good and that is God Himself. Jesus refused to let anyone patronize Him by calling Him a "great moral teacher" or "a good man." C. S. Lewis explained the situation this way:

> A man who was merely a man and said the sort of things Jesus said would not be a great moral teacher. He would either be a lunatic— on a level with the man who says he is a poached egg—or He would be the Devil of Hell. You must make a choice. Either this man was, and is, the Son of God; or else a madman or something worse ... But let us not come with any patronising nonsense about His being a great human teacher. He has not left that open to us. He did not intend to.[2]

Liar, lunatic—or Lord. Those are our only choices. If Jesus is good, He is God; if Jesus is not God, He is not good.

In John 8:46, Jesus asked His opponents, "Which of you convinceth [convicts] me of sin?" The answer: none of them. His enemies could find no crime of which to accuse Him. Even more telling, those who walked with Him daily and observed His life up close also knew He was a sinless man. Judas, who betrayed Him, said, "I have sinned in that I have betrayed the innocent blood" (Matt. 27:4). The man who had the power to condemn Him, Pontius Pilate, also said, "I find no fault in this man" (Luke 23:4). The repenting thief who died on the cross next to Him said, "We receive the due reward of our deeds: but this man hath done nothing amiss" (Luke 23:41). The centurion who thrust the spear into His side said, "Certainly this was a righteous man" (Luke 23:47). Clearly, Jesus is good. Why? Because *Jesus is God.*

The closer a person comes to Jesus, the more clearly that person sees his or her own imperfections and sin in contrast to His sinless perfection. This was true of Peter, who said to Jesus, "Depart from me; for I am a sinful man, O Lord" (Luke 5:8). It was true of Paul, who declared himself to be the chief of sinners.

This was also true of Augustine, who is known as Saint Augustine today. I doubt that he would like being known as Saint Augustine, for he was such a humble man, so aware of his own sin, that he would probably consider himself the least among believers. Have you ever heard of his book called *The Virtues of St. Augustine*? Of course you haven't—and you never will! Augustine never wrote a book of virtues; he wrote a book of confessions. *The Confessions of St. Augustine* is an honest and humble catalog of his own wretchedness and sinfulness.

There is another book you have never read and never will: *The Confessions of Jesus*. That book does not exist. If such a book were ever published, it would be blank on every page. Why? Because Jesus Christ could say, "Which of you convinceth me of sin?" Though all others have sinned and come short of the glory of God, Jesus never sinned.

Today He asks us: "Who do you say that I am?" And we must answer. The answer the Bible gives is clear and unmistakable: Jesus Christ is God. If you go to the first chapter of Genesis and look at the first words, you find this statement: "In the beginning God created the heavens and the earth" (Gen. 1:1). The Hebrew word translated "God" is *Elohim*, which is a plural form. There is also a singular form for the word "God," *El*, but in Genesis 1, the word used for God is the plural form, *Elohim*. So this statement could reasonably, literally, be translated, "In the beginning, *Gods* created the heavens and the earth."

I am not saying that there are many Gods. There is one God, but that God has a plural nature—three personalities in one God. We find the plural nature of God clearly expressed a little further in the same chapter, where God said, "Let *us* make man in *our* image, after *our* likeness" (Gen. 1:26, emphasis added). Who is this "Us"? Clearly, it is the Persons (plural) that make up the Godhead (singular).

So this is the essence of the God of the Old Testament—a God who is both singular and plural. How many persons? The Old Testament does not say—but in the New Testament, the nature of God becomes much more clear: There is but one God, and that one God exists in three Persons—Father, Son, and Holy Spirit. We see this singular/plural nature of God in Matthew 28:19, where Jesus commands us to baptize people in the name (singular) of the Father, and the Son, and the Holy Spirit—one name, three Persons.

How does God the Father address God the Son? In Hebrews 1:8, we catch a glimpse into that relationship. There we read:

> But unto the Son he saith, Thy throne, O God, is for ever and ever: a
> sceptre of righteousness is the sceptre of thy kingdom.

Here, God clearly calls Jesus "God." It doesn't get any clearer than that. Those who would say that Jesus, being the Son of God, is not truly God simply have not read or do not understand the Scriptures. Jesus is not a sub-God or a semi-God. He is fully God. He and God the Father are one. As God says in Isaiah 46:9:

> For I am God, and there is none else; I am God, and there is none like
> me.

But it is not only the claims of Jesus and of Scripture that convince us that He is God. Simply by examining His life, we see that Jesus was clearly a unique Person—a *divine* personality. We date our calendars according to the life of this Man, yet there is no earthly explanation for His greatness. He grew up in an insignificant village in a conquered and beaten nation. There was a saying about the town in which He lived: "Can any good thing come out of Nazareth?" He labored in obscurity for the first thirty years of His life, toiling in a carpenter's shop, far from universities, libraries, and centers of economic and political power of His time—yet He became the wisest of the wise.

Known for His meekness and humility, He called Himself "greater than Solomon" (Matt. 12:42). Such a statement would be the height of egotism and folly for you or me. But when Jesus spoke those words, they seemed fitting and right. Wherever He went, people marveled at His wisdom. "How knoweth this man letters, having never learned?" (John 7:15)—that is, how did He become so learned and wise without a formal education?

But the answer to their question is self-evident, isn't it? God would hardly need to *study* in order to know all there is to know! What could a university teach the Creator of the universe? What could the greatest library in the world teach the living Word of God? There is nothing God needs to learn. He is the Source of all knowledge and all truth. So even though Jesus emerged from obscurity, without education or degrees, He was wise beyond all human wisdom, because He was Wisdom itself. Jesus, the Son of God, is fully God in every way.

When Jesus emerged from obscurity, walked up on a mountain, and delivered the greatest oration on human ethics the world had ever heard, it was the Creator God, standing upon a mountain of His own making, on a planet of His own design, delivering insights into spiritual and moral realities that He Himself had authored. No wonder those who heard His teachings were astonished. Why? Because the wisdom that proceeded from His lips was literally the wisdom of Almighty God Himself!

The wisdom of Jesus was totally unlike the wisdom of the greatest and wisest men of His time—or of any other time. It is well known that the wisest philosophers of Greece and Rome condoned all manner of evil, such as slavery, oppression, revenge, infanticide, polygamy, concubinage, and other vices. And not only did they condone those things, but they also practiced many such vices themselves. But the teaching of Jesus and the life of Jesus were on a totally different plane than the so-called wisdom of the pagans. He not only taught an unheard-of message, but He also lived it to absolute perfection.

A WALKING ASTONISHMENT

It is interesting that most people today think that the teachings of Jesus are the essence of Christianity—but that is not so. The teachings of Jesus are secondary to Christianity. You might be surprised to discover that the apostle Paul says almost nothing about the teachings of Jesus in his letters, which make up most of the New Testament. Not one of Jesus' parables is mentioned. In fact, throughout the rest of the New Testament there is little reference to the teachings of Jesus.

In the Apostles' Creed, that most universally held Christian creed, there is no reference to the teachings of Jesus, nor is there any reference to the example of Jesus. The creed states, in part:

> I believe in God, the Father Almighty,
> Maker of Heaven and Earth,
> And in Jesus Christ, His only Son, our Lord,
> Who was conceived by the Holy Spirit,
> Born of the Virgin Mary,
> Suffered under Pontius Pilate,
> Was crucified, dead, and buried . . .

Notice that this portion of the ancient creed mentions only two days in the life of Jesus: the day of His birth and the day of His death. Why? Because Christianity is not centered on the teachings of Christ (as important as they certainly are), but on the *Person* of Jesus as the incarnate God who came into this world to take upon Himself our guilt and to die in our place.

This is utterly astonishing when you think about it. Can you imagine a biography of any other person that told you about the day he was born, with the next chapter telling you about the day that he died, and nothing in between? Why does the Apostles' Creed tell His story this way? It is because Jesus Christ, unlike any other person that ever was born, was *born to die*. He was slain in the mind of God before the creation of the universe, before the foundation of the world. That's why He came: He came to die. He came to pay a debt He didn't owe because we owed a debt we couldn't pay.

Jesus Christ—unlike all of the founders of all the other religions of the world—died for the sins of the world. No other person ever considered or thought about or talked about dying for the sins of the world. Who could ever consider such a thing? Who would be pure and holy enough to pay such a price except God Himself? We can't even pay for our own sins, short of Hell. How could you or I pay for the sins of the entire world, for those who came before us centuries ago, and for those who will come after us, and for those we don't even know? Jesus is unique. While the founders of other religions died peacefully in their beds, Jesus died ignominiously, agonizingly, excruciatingly upon the cruel cross of Calvary.

Christ stands apart from all of the founders of the world's religions. He solved the fundamental human problem—the problem of sin. The sin problem exists untouched by any founder of any other religion. It is the problem that keeps mankind out of Heaven and sends millions to Hell. No one else is good enough or pure enough or mighty enough to pay the penalty for sin—only Christ alone. Christianity is unlike every other religion on earth because its Founder died to pay for the sins of mankind.

Christianity is also unlike every other religion in that Jesus alone, of all of the founders of all the religions of the world, *rose from the dead.* I have visited the tombs of many of the founders of religious sects around the world. You can travel the Mediterranean region and find numerous sites where pieces of Muhammad are enshrined. They have a tooth here and a finger there and the rest of him elsewhere. But if you go into the tomb of Christ, you will find that it is empty. Visit the tomb of Buddha or Confucius, and you will find a corpse and an inscription: "Here lie the mortal remains of . . ."

But what do you encounter at the tomb of Jesus? Only what the visitors to that tomb encountered on the first Easter morning: a voice saying, "He is not here: for he is risen, as he said" (Matt. 28:6). And only Jesus Christ offers many infallible proofs (as Luke says in Acts 1:3) that He rose from the dead and was seen and touched and heard by more than five hundred witnesses for almost six weeks. He ate with them, walked with them, talked with them, and showed Himself to be alive from the dead.

The great agonizing question that has been wrenched from the hearts of millions of people down through the centuries is that question from the oldest book of the Bible: "If a man die, shall he live again?" (Job 14:14) For centuries that question was always answered in the depressing and hopeless negative. But Jesus changed the answer from a forlorn "no" to a triumphant "yes!" He alone can say, "I am he that liveth, and was dead; and, behold, I am alive for evermore" (Rev. 1:18).

THE JESUS OF THE GOSPELS
IS THE HISTORICAL JESUS

The Bible tells us that "we have this treasure in earthen vessels" (2 Cor. 4:7). What is this treasure? According to the preceding verse, it is "the knowledge of the glory of God," as revealed in Jesus Christ. And who or what are the earthen vessels? We are!

When I was in seminary, one of the first things my professors taught me was, "Don't preach yourself! You are an earthen vessel! The Gospel message is the treasure, not you!" Woe unto the poor congregation whose preacher is always talking about himself! Woe to the poor congregation whose preacher always wants to sing his favorite hymn, "How Great I Am"! Such a preacher should be looked upon with pity, if not utter contempt—if that preacher is a mere human being.

But what if that preacher is Jesus? He preached Himself all of the time! Jesus Christ did something that no other preacher or founder of any religion has ever done: He founded His religion upon Himself. He said, "I am the way, the truth, and the life" (John 14:6). He said, "I am the resurrection, and the life" (John 11:25). Jesus constantly preached about Himself. And for Him to do so would be the height of arrogance and, yes, blasphemy—*if He had not been God!*

But being God, there was no greater message that He could possibly preach than Himself. And that is exactly what He preached. As you read through the Gospels, you discover something fascinating about His message: Jesus didn't urge people to come to God. He urged people to come to *Himself.* And He preached Himself in a way that seemed perfectly natural and even humble. Why? Because Jesus is God. And since He is truly God, then it is perfectly natural for Him to preach Himself! What greater message could He possibly bring to the people but the message of Himself?

Jesus went about doing good. He didn't just give a message of comfort to the poor or a word of encouragement to the sick. He worked miracles! He raised the dead, enabled the lame to walk, and opened the eyes of the blind. He unstopped the ears of the deaf and loosened the tongues of the dumb. This Man was a walking astonishment!

And yet, I've heard it said many times, "Well, that's just what the Bible says about Jesus. How do we know what the *real, historical* Jesus actually did and said?" But even skeptics have to confess that the Jesus of the Gospels is much more than a mythological creation. How could a bunch of illiterate fisherman from first-century Palestine have created such a dynamic, wise, insightful, astounding, forceful personality as Jesus Christ? The suggestion that Jesus is a mere myth is simply unthinkable.

Moreover, we have much more than the Gospel writings to go on in our understanding of the historical Jesus. Among the secular writers of antiquity who wrote about Him are Tacitus, the great Roman historian; Suetonius, another historian; Pliny the younger; Epictus; Lucian; Aristides; Galenus; Lampridius; DioCassius; Hinnerius; Libanius; Ammianus; Marcellinus; Euniapius; Zosimus. Others wrote whole books about Christ: Celsus, Porphyry, Hierocles, and Julian the Apostate. And many Jewish writers of Jesus' time, such as Josephus, also wrote about Christ. When we boil it all down, it becomes evident that the Jesus of the Gospels *is* the historical Jesus. Those who seek any other Jesus are chasing a figment of their own imaginations.

The power of Jesus' personality generates awe, admiration, and worship, even across the centuries. It jumps out from the pages of Scripture and seizes the minds and hearts of believers and skeptics alike. In fact, many skeptics who investigate Christ with the intent of debunking Him end up praising Him—and committing their lives to Him.

One such person was General Lew Wallace, an agnostic with a legal and literary background. An atheist friend once told Wallace that within a few years, all the little white churches that dotted the Indiana countryside where they lived would be nothing but a memory. Christianity, said Wallace's friend, was in decline and would soon collapse. He challenged Wallace to use his literary talents to write a book presenting Jesus as a mere man among men, not the Son of God. Wallace knew little about the Christian faith, so he decided to read the Bible for himself and make up his own mind. He believed his trained, logical, legal mind would enable him to sort out fact from fantasy in the story of Jesus Christ.

As he studied the New Testament, Lew Wallace gradually came to the conclusion that Jesus was no ordinary man—that He was, in fact, God in the flesh. Wallace became a Christian and wrote a novel that presented Jesus as the divine Son of God. Two different movie versions of his novel were filmed. The title of his novel: *Ben-Hur!* [3]

Those who honestly examine the life of Christ come away convinced that He is no ordinary man, but the God–man. Historian Philip

Schaff of Yale testifies, "The person of Christ is to me the greatest and surest of all facts; as certain as my own personal existence—nay, more certain am I of Christ than I am of my own personal existence."

German novelist Johann Paul Friedrich Richter (1763–1825), author of *Hesperus* and *Titan*, said of Jesus, "He is the purest among the mighty, the mightiest among the pure," a Man who "lifted with His pierced hands empires off their hinges and turned the stream of centuries out of its channel and still governs the ages."

The famous French skeptic Ernest Renan (1823–1892) lost his faith at age twenty-two while preparing for the Catholic priesthood. He wrote many books critical of the Bible and the Christian faith, including *Vie de Jesus* (*The Life of Jesus*), a skeptical examination of the Lord's ministry on earth. Though he rejected the supernatural and miraculous explanation of Jesus' life, Renan could not explain away the power of His teaching and His personality. At the end of his biography of Christ, Renan concluded: "Whatever may be the surprises of the future, Jesus will not be surpassed . . . All the ages will proclaim that among the sons of men there is none born who is greater than Jesus."

And consider the testimony of Napoleon Bonaparte, the French emperor and military genius. After his defeat at Waterloo, Napoleon was exiled to the island of St. Helena. Stripped of his former office and his former power, he had a great deal of time on his hands, so he studied the Bible. The more Napoleon studied, the more astonished he was at Christ. He once said to one of his generals who was with him in exile:

> I know men; and I tell you, Jesus Christ is not a man. Superficial minds see a resemblance between Christ and the founders of empires, and the gods of other religions. That resemblance does not exist. There is between Christianity and whatever other religions the distance of infinity.[4]

We can say to the authors of every other religion: "You are neither gods nor the agents of deity, but you are propagandists of falsehood, molded from the same clay as the rest of mortal humanity. You are made with all of the same passions and vices of all other human beings. Your temples and your priests proclaim your all-too-human origin. Jesus alone is the God–Man."

The death of Jesus is the death of God. This view has been held by some of the greatest thinkers of the last two thousand years. Christ is unique because: (1) He is God; and (2) He is the only perfect person who ever existed. There is no fault to be found in Him.

So we return to the original mystery, the core question, of this chapter: Is Jesus God—or the Son of God? People have put that very question to me on various occasions—"How can Jesus be God when the Scripture says that He is the Son of God?" The question I always ask in return is this: "Does the Bible call Jesus the Lamb of God?" And if they have any knowledge of the Scripture at all, they will say, "Yes, the Bible does call Him that." (If they do not know, I simply open my Bible to such passages as John 1:29, Revelation 5:12, and a number of other references to Christ as the Lamb.) Then I say, "But that can't be. Jesus can't be the Lamb of God. The Bible calls Him the Good Shepherd. He can't be a Lamb and a Shepherd at the same time!" And then, usually, they see the error of their thinking.

The fact is, Jesus can be many things at once. He is the Door to eternal life—and He is the One who stands at the door of our hearts and knocks. He is the Way, the Truth, and the Life. He is the Good Shepherd. He is the Lamb of God. He is the Lion of Judah. He is the Son of God. And He is almighty God Himself. There is no contradiction in these varied descriptions, only completeness.

The brilliant minds of this world—those who have taken an honest and unbiased look at Christ—have seen the glory of Christ, a glory that transcends and far exceeds any mere human wisdom or intellect. Jesus was fully man, but He was not merely man. He is (in the words of the confession that was wrenched from the trembling lips of the doubting disciple, Thomas) our Lord and our God!

Who is this Jesus? He is omnipresent, omniscient, almighty, and unchangeable. He created the universe, and by Him the universe is upheld from one moment to the next. He is the object of all our desiring and our worship. He and the Father are one. If we have seen Jesus, we have seen God the Father. And this is the One who offers Himself as your Savior. The Creator Himself came and died for the sins of His creatures—your sins and mine.

I shall never forget the day I realized just who Jesus is. For two thousand years He had been reaching down with pierced hands and a loving heart, lifting broken and twisted souls out of the mire of sin—but I thought I had no need of Him. Then I happened to read a simple book, a novel based on the life of Jesus, *The Greatest Story Ever Told* by Fulton Oursler. I had started reading that book as a mere historical novel, never imagining how it would transform my life. The story of Jesus was so powerful that, even in a novel form, it reached out and seized my mind and my heart. I was touched by His teaching, but I was overwhelmed by His love. I was in agony as He suffered and died upon the cross. And I was exultant as He stepped forth from the tomb in resurrection power.

When I closed the book and laid it down upon the arm of the easy chair, it seemed that I could see the cross of Christ standing before me. I slid out of my chair and fell to my knees. Weeping uncontrollably, I put my forehead on the carpet and cried, "O God, I didn't know! I didn't know! I am sorry! I am so, so sorry! Please forgive me!"

And my heart was changed in that very moment. I became a new creature in Jesus Christ. That was forty-five years ago, and He gets better all the time. He is my Lord and my God, my Savior and my Friend.

Do you know Him? Have you personally met Him, invited Him into your heart as Lord and Savior of your life? If not, dear friend, you are missing the greatest thing in the world. I urge you to say yes to Him. Make Jesus not only your Savior, not only your Lord, but make Him the almighty God of your life!

THE MYSTERY OF THE TRINITY: HOW CAN GOD BE BOTH *THREE* AND *ONE*?

Let me pose a mystery to you. I don't think you'll have much trouble solving it. Here is the mystery for you to solve:

$$1 + 1 + 1 = \underline{\hspace{1.5in}}$$

Take your time. Use a piece of scratch paper if you need to. No, it's not a trick question. Do you have the solution? If the answer you get is 3, then you have solved this little mystery.

Anyone who has progressed beyond first grade should be able to figure out that one. In fact, some people have used this simple mathematical exercise to "prove" the "impossibility" of the Trinity, the biblical concept that our God is *one* God in *three* Persons. Critics claim that we Christians, who believe in the Trinity, are saying that $1 + 1 + 1 = 1$. The fact is, all this proves is that those who reject the Trinity do not understand the Trinity.

Christians have never taught that $1 + 1 + 1 = 1$. Whenever someone confronts me with this mathematical logic in an effort to disprove the Trinity, I reply, "There's only one thing wrong with your mathematical reasoning, my friend."

"Oh?" comes the usual response. "What's that?"

"You are applying the wrong equation. You should not ask, 'What is 1 + 1 + 1?' Instead, the question should be, 'What is 1 x 1 x 1?' What would your answer be to that question?"

Gulp! "Well—it would be one."

Exactly. We make a great mistake in attempting to understand the Trinity if we view God as three "somethings" adding up to a sum. God is not a cherry pie divided up in three pieces. The Father, the Son, and the Holy Spirit are not each one-third of a God. Each is fully God. One times One times One equals One.

God is One, and God is three. He is One in a very different sense from the sense in which He is three. He is One in His spiritual essence. He is three in the distinction between the three personalities within the Godhead. So there is no mathematical confusion or logical absurdity at all. Yes, God's nature is a mystery we cannot fully comprehend, but it is not an absurdity that we cannot logically accept. The reality of God is mysterious, but rational and deeply beautiful.

A FOUNDATIONAL CHRISTIAN TRUTH

The Trinity is not a side issue. It is not a theological fine point. It is the foundation of all Christian doctrine, the substratum upon which the great superstructure rests. You cannot understand the Christian religion unless you understand the Trinity, because a misunderstanding of the Trinity inevitably creates distortion in our understanding of every other doctrine of the Christian faith. If you do not understand the Trinity, you will not understand the deity of Christ, the meaning of the Incarnation, the substitutionary atonement of Christ upon the cross, the meaning of the Resurrection, the doctrine of justification by faith, and on and on!

All Christian worship begins and ends with the Trinity. It is the summation of the doxology that is sung in churches worldwide every Lord's Day:

Praise *God,* from whom all blessings flow;

Praise Him, all creatures here below;

Praise Him above, ye heavenly host;

Praise *Father, Son,* and *Holy Ghost* (emphasis added).[1]

All Christian worship revolves around the doctrine of the Trinity. And if we err in the foundation, we will err in all other Christian doctrines. If the foundation is not firm, our structure will be unstable. If we are unfaithful to the biblical truth of the Trinity, we open ourselves to heresy and spiritual error in every other point of the Christian faith, for the Trinity is the distinctive mark of Christianity.

No other belief system has any concept like the Trinity. True, there are "triads" in various religions, such as the Hindu triad of Brahma, Vishnu, and Shiva, or the ancient Egyptian triad of Isis, Osirus, and Horus. But these are simply trios of independent deities. The Christian Trinity is distinct in its subtle mystery of threeness and oneness. Every other religion in the world either worships a solitary deity or a pantheon of many gods. (The roll call of Hindu deities is estimated at as many as three million gods!) The Trinity takes the truth of both of two opposed errors and combines them into one great and beautiful reality: God is One, and God is three.

I am often surprised at the way some people try to make the Trinity understandable in simple terms. Some have tried to suggest that the Trinity is like water that may exist as a liquid, a solid, or a gas. This image is meant to clarify the trinitarian concept, but only succeeds in obscuring the reality of the Trinity! While it is true that water can take three forms, it can only exist in one form at a time—but God exists as three Persons at all times!

Others have tried to get around the reality of the Trinity by suggesting that there is only one personal God, and that is God the Father. The Son, they say, was not truly God, but merely a highly exalted, spiritually attuned human being—a great creature, but not a Creator. And the Holy Spirit? They say that the Spirit is an impersonal force—the active and dynamic force that God the Father uses to accomplish His will. Many cults hold to such a view.

Still others have likened the Trinity to a person having three roles. So, for example, when I step into the pulpit, I am a pastor; when I step into my home, I'm a husband and father; when I step onto a crosswalk, I'm a pedestrian. One person, three roles. But this analogy doesn't bring us any closer to the truth of the Trinity. In fact, it leads us into an ancient heresy known as Modalist Monarchianism or Sabellianism (after the African-Roman priest, Sabellius, who proposed the idea). Sabellianists believed that the Father, Son, and Holy Spirit were just different modes or guises of the same Monarch (hence Modalist Monarchianism). In this heresy, God the Monarch appeared first as the Father; then He went behind the scene and changed His costume, reappearing as the Son; then He disappeared again to emerge once more as the Holy Spirit.

But that is not the view of the Trinity we find in the Bible. The Godhead is eternally and always made up of three distinct Persons of equal power and glory. These three Persons are equally worshipped by Christians throughout the ages. All efforts to reduce the Trinity to a Unity lead ultimately to heresy, cultism, and false religion.

The great Presbyterian theologian, Charles Hodge, said this about the Unitarian (one God, one Person) concept of God, which is found not only in Unitarianism, but also in Islam and Judaism:

A Unitarian, one-personed God might possibly have existed, and if revealed as such, it would have been our duty to have acknowledged His lordship. But, nevertheless, He would have always remained utterly inconceivable to us—one lone, fellowless conscious being; subject without object; conscious person without environment; righteous being without fellowship or moral relation or sphere of right action. Where would there be to Him a sphere of love, truth, trust, or sympathetic feeling? Before creation, eternal darkness: after creation, only an endless game of solitaire with worlds for pawns.

No, the concept of a lone single-person as God existing from all eternity, all by Himself, is something we creatures who live in families with friends find very difficult to understand.

The Westminster Confession of Faith, which embodies the doctrines of the Presbyterian faith, states:

There is but one only, living, and true God . . . In the unity of the Godhead there be three Persons of one substance, power, and eternity: God the Father, God the Son, and God the Holy Ghost. The Father is of none, neither begotten, nor proceeding: the Son is eternally begotten of the Father; the Holy Ghost eternally proceeding from the Father and the Son.

The matter of being eternally begotten or eternally proceeding as the Son from the Father does not mean that the Father was prior to the Son, which is the Western way of thinking of father–son relationships. Our cultural tendency is to view the father as the source, existing prior to the son. But in the Eastern or Semitic way of thinking, that is not the emphasis. Instead, the father–son relationship emphasizes likeness or sameness—the sharing of an identical essence or nature.

Those who reject the truth of the Trinity usually do so out of a misunderstanding of what the Trinity really means. Muslims sometimes accuse Christians of worshipping three Gods. But the Bible does not present three Gods—just one. That one God is complex, and comprised of three distinct Personalities, three distinct centers or sources of knowledge: will, consciousness, and love. These three Personalities share the same nature and essence and power—but they are not each the same Personality. So there is a richness and beautiful diversity within the unity that is God. This is the teaching of Scripture, and it has been the historic view of the Church in all of its branches down through the centuries. All the great creeds of Christendom embrace the triune concept of God.

THE TRINITY IN SCRIPTURE

The doctrine of the Trinity does not rest on a few isolated verses of Scripture, ripped out of context. It is woven into the fabric of Scripture, embedded upon every page. The nineteenth-century English minister Edward Bickersteth conducted an intense study of the subject, finding literally hundreds of Scripture passages that affirm the doctrine of the Trinity. Though the Trinity is often alluded to in the Old Testament, it is interesting to note that the trinitarian concept is fully revealed only in the New Testament. Why do you suppose that is? Why didn't God reveal His triune nature in the Old Testament? I believe the answer is two-fold:

1. There was no need for the Trinity to be revealed until the Son was sent forth to carry out the plan of salvation. When Jesus came to become the atonement for our sins through His death upon the cross; when He was raised again and went back to the Father; and when they together sent the Holy Spirit to us to regenerate and sanctify us—only when all of these things were accomplished was it necessary for God to reveal the inmost secrets of the divine nature. The Trinity was revealed not so much by words, but by the act of Jesus' entrance into the world. We do not believe in the deity of Christ because we believe in the Trinity; rather, we believe in the Trinity because we are convinced beyond any doubt that Jesus is truly God in human form.

2. In the Old Testament, when God set apart the Israelites as His chosen people, He knew it would be necessary to safeguard them against the false doctrines of polytheism. The Israelites lived in a pagan world, surrounded by false polytheistic religions and in constant danger of corruption. So God impressed upon their minds the truth of monotheism: there is only one God. In their worship services, the Israelites proclaimed (and still proclaim to this day) what is called the Shema, taken from Deuteronomy 6:4: "Hear, O Israel: The LORD our God is one LORD."

Even so, there are foreshadowings of God's triune nature in the Old

Testament. The New Testament is, of course, a more advanced, more complete revelation because the revelation of God gradually progresses and unfolds from Genesis all the way through the book of Revelation. But as we saw in the previous chapter, God is clearly presented as a plural being from the very first verse in Genesis. Some have suggested that when God speaks in the first-person plural (as in Gen. 1:26: "Let us make man in our image, after our likeness"), He is simply using the "royal we," the "majestic plural," as when Queen Victoria said, "We are not amused." But even assuming that the Creator God, at the beginning of time, was in the habit of talking to Himself in the manner of a nineteenth-century British monarch, that does not explain the many times in the Old Testament that God is referred to in the plural form.

We see God taking counsel within His own plural self not only in the creation story, but also in the story of the Fall, in Genesis 3:22, where Jehovah God says, "Behold, the man is become as one of us, to know good and evil." Someone has suggested that God is talking to the angels. But if so, why are angels not mentioned in this context? But even more importantly, this suggestion ignores the fact that angels are not the counselors or advisors of God. He never takes counsel of the angels, only of Himself. He commands angels, and they serve Him.

We see the plural nature of God again in Genesis 11:7, where God says: "Go to, let *us* go down [to the Tower of Babel], and there confound their language, that they may not understand one another's speech" (emphasis added). In fact, throughout the Old Testament we see God referred to in singular, then plural, then singular terms again. In fact, we find both singular and plural in a single verse, Isaiah 6:8, wherein God says, "Whom shall I [singular] send, and who will go for us [plural]?"

I think it is fascinating that even the Shema, the bedrock foundation of Old Testament monotheism, which Jews repeat every Sabbath—"Hear, O Israel: The LORD our God is one LORD"—uses a particular Hebrew word for "one." That word is *achad*, which means "a one of unity." It is a word that is used for a cluster of grapes—an *achad* of grapes, "a number of objects joined into a unified whole."

If the plural nature of God is so strongly indicated in the Old Testament, why have the Jewish people so strongly resisted the concept of the Trinity? Leopold Cohn, a former rabbi who came to know Jesus as His Messiah and Savior in 1894, and who died in 1936, observed that one of the reasons Jews cannot grasp and accept the tri-unity of God is due to the teachings of their greatest theologian, Moses Maimonides. Often called "the Second Moses," he lived in the twelfth century and compiled a creed that the Jews incorporated into their liturgy and that is repeated in virtually every synagogue in the world today:

> I believe with a perfect faith that the Creator, blessed be His name, is an *absolute one.*

The Hebrew word that Moses Maimonides chose for "absolute one," says Cohn, is *yachid*, meaning "a single, solitary, indivisible one." That is a very different word from *achad*, the word that God, speaking through the first Moses, selected when He inspired the writing of the Shema in Deuteronomy 6:4. Rabbi Cohn described some of the other ways *achad* is used in Scripture. For example, Genesis 1:5, which describes the first day of creation, concludes (in a literal translation from the Hebrew), "And there was evening and there was morning, one day." The word "one" is *achad*, not *yachid*. This verse suggests plurality within unity, the unity of evening and morning into one (*achad*) day. And again, in Genesis 2:24, we read: "Therefore shall a man leave his father and his mother, and shall cleave unto his wife: and they shall be one flesh." In marriage, two distinct personalities become one (*achad*) flesh, one union of two souls.

When the word *yachid* appears in Scripture, it always means a single and solitary one, as in Genesis 22:2, where God tells Abraham, "Take now thy son, thine only [*yachid*] son Isaac," or Zechariah 12:10: "and they shall look upon me whom they have pierced, and they shall mourn for him, as one mourneth for his only [*yachid*] son." But *yachid* is not the word used of Jehovah. He is not *yachid*, a single, solitary one; He is *achad*, a One that is a unity of essence but a diversity of personalities. By applying a word to God that Scripture never applies to Him, Moses Maimonides misled his people and blinded them to the beautiful truth of God's full, rich nature.

When we come to the New Testament, however, the light is turned on and the Scriptures fairly sparkle with the teaching of the Trinity. We don't have to look at a few isolated texts. The Trinity saturates every page. Wherever the New Testament underscores the deity of Christ, or wherever it mentions the personality and ministry of the Holy Spirit, we find an embedded, implicit, yet unmistakable reference to God's triune nature.

When John 1:1 tells us, "In the beginning was the Word, and the Word was with God, and the Word was God," we are getting a lesson in the nature of the Trinity. When Thomas falls on his knees before the risen Christ, exclaiming, "My Lord and my God!" we are witnessing one man's dramatic encounter with God's triune reality. When we read in the New Testament about the Person of the Holy Spirit—not a force or an inanimate power, but a Person who sends and acts and wills and directs, a Person who loves and encourages and who can be grieved—we are discovering yet another aspect of the Trinity.

The three Persons of the Trinity are often given an order—First, Second, and Third Person—not because one is greater than another, but because of a beautiful ordering of activity that takes place within the Trinity. God the Father is said to be the First Person of the Trinity; God the Son is the Second; God the Spirit is the Third. This is the order in which the Persons are introduced to us in Scripture. In the Old Testament we see God primarily as a Father (though hints of the Son and Spirit are liberally sprinkled throughout the Old Testament). With the arrival of Christ in the New Testament, we are fully introduced to the Second Person of the Trinity. And when He ascends to the Father, He and the Father jointly send to us the Third Person of the Trinity, the Holy Spirit.

As the eternally existent God, Jesus is equal to God the Father in every way, but (as Philippians 2:6–8 tells us) He willingly chose to empty Himself of the prerogatives of Godhood and take the form of a servant, the likeness of a mere man. As a man, He subjected Himself to the Father and said, "My Father is greater than I" (John 14:28). This does not mean that God the Son is lower than God the Father in any way. It only means that, for a period of time, Jesus willingly submitted Himself to the Father.

We witness the activity of the three Persons of the Trinity at the baptism of Jesus, Matthew 3:13–17. There we see Jesus, the Second Person, being baptized; we see the Spirit of God, the Third Person, descending like a dove; and we hear the voice of the Father, the First Person, claiming Jesus as His own Son. Jesus Himself described the three Persons of the Trinity in John 15:26, where He said, "But when the Comforter is come, whom I will send unto you from the Father, even the Spirit of truth [the Third Person], which proceedeth from the Father [the First Person], he shall testify of me [the Second Person]." And Paul, in Ephesians 1:17 (NKJV), wrote, "I keep asking that the God of our Lord Jesus Christ [the Second Person], the Father of glory [the First Person], may give unto you the Spirit [the Third Person] of wisdom and revelation: in the knowledge of him." I could fill the pages of this book with examples. In verse after verse, the same truth is taught: We worship a great triune God.

THE PRACTICAL TRUTH OF THE TRINITY

What are the functions of the three Persons of the Trinity? Since each is a unique personality, each has specific roles and tasks to perform. Yes, the Father permeates the Son and the Spirit, and the Son permeates the Father and the Spirit. Yes, as Jesus said, "I am in the Father, and the Father in me" (John 14:11). But the Father, the Son, and the Holy Spirit also have specific functions.

The tasks of the Father are essentially these: (1) creation of the universe; (2) election of believers (see Mystery 3: "Which Is True—Predestination or Free Will?"); and (3) authorship of the plan of salvation and redemption (it was the Father's plan to send the Son).

The tasks of the Son are essentially these: (1) becoming incarnate in human form and living a perfectly holy life; (2) suffering an atoning death upon the cross; and (3) rising victoriously from the dead.

The tasks of the Holy Spirit are essentially these: (1) regenerating us by indwelling us at the moment of salvation; (2) sanctifying us and setting us apart for His service; and (3) coming alongside us as a Comforter in times of sorrow, trouble, and distress.

This is God in both His splendid oneness and His diversity, His manifold and multifaceted unity. And unless you understand who God is, you cannot truly understand the Christian faith. There are many people, of course, who believe in God without believing in the Trinity. But they have scarcely grasped the fringe of the garment of God. They have only the tiniest inkling of the much more grand and profound reality of God. What a tragedy it is to willfully ignore and bypass this profound truth—a truth that can be so easily discovered by simply opening the pages of the Bible.

Jesus said that knowing God is the essence of eternal life. "And this is life eternal, that they might know thee the only true God, and Jesus Christ, whom thou hast sent" (John 17:3). So if you don't know God— if you don't grasp the fullness of His three distinct but unified Personalities—you are missing out on the rich reward of eternal life! If you worship a God who is a lone, solitary God, then you are worshipping some God other than the Christian God.

Do not make the mistake of thinking that the matter of the Trinity is a mere issue of lofty theological debate. This is an intensely practical and personal issue for every Christian. The reality of the Trinity has an immediate and far-reaching impact on our everyday lives. Let me suggest three ways in which this takes place:

1. Each Person in the Trinity has a specific role to play in our lives. I would encourage you to meditate upon the work of each of these Persons. Think about what God the Father did for you in placing you within His wonderful creation, in electing you to salvation, and in authoring the plan to redeem you from your sin. Think about the work of God the Son in His incarnation, His crucifixion, and His resurrection. Think about the work of the Holy Spirit in regenerating you, in making you alive from the deadness of your sin, in sanctifying and cleansing you day by day, and in comforting you in times of sorrow and pain. God will bless your life as you meditate upon what He has done for you through each of His three Persons.

2. *We can pray to each Person of the Trinity.* Though it is true that we normally pray to the Father in the name of the Son and in the power of the Holy Spirit, there are other kinds of prayers recorded in the Scriptures. Within the New Testament there are prayers directed to the Father, prayers directed to the Son, and prayers directed to the Holy Spirit. We can pray to each Person, for all three are equal in power and glory. Your prayer life may be enriched as you address each Person of the Trinity, remembering what each has done in your life.

3. *The reality of the Trinity guarantees our salvation.* If there is no Trinity, then Jesus is not God, but merely a man. And if Jesus is not God, then He cannot be our Redeemer. The Bible makes it clear that no mere sinful human being could ever pay the price for sin. Only a perfect sacrifice, a divine sacrifice, is sufficient. Nearly a thousand years ago, Saint Anselm, the Archbishop of Canterbury, said, "The sin of the world is an infinite sin and requires an infinite penalty—and who shall pay it? The Redeemer must be an infinite One."

Furthermore, it is man who has sinned, not angels or oxen or sheep or goats. So it is man who must pay the penalty. The price must be paid by a Man—but not any man, only a perfect Man, an infinite Man, a God–Man. It is only because of the infinite merit of the atonement of the God–Man upon the cross that you and I can be saved. Deny the Trinity, and you deny any hope of atonement for your sin. Deny the Trinity, and you remain in your sin.

Because of the Trinity, you can know that you are loved by God. The Scripture makes plain that the essence of God is love.

Long before the creation of the universe, our triune God was perfect and complete in love. The Father, Son, and Spirit existed as One, communing together in love and fellowship, lacking nothing. God did not create angels and human beings in order to fulfill some lack or emptiness in His personality. God is love, and God is perfect. The creation we inhabit, and even our existence, is a gift of sheer grace from a perfect and complete God of love.

If you have never met this wondrous triune God, my prayer for you is that you will come to experience Him in all three of His Persons. When you come to know Jesus Christ, you are made into a new creation. You are fashioned by the hand of the triune God into His very image as He daily changes you and molds you, giving you the assurance and certainty that you are on your way to heaven. My prayer for you, my friend, is:

- that you will find God the Son as your Lord and Savior

- that you will experience God the Spirit as your Companion and Comforter

- that you will discover God the Father as your Maker and Master, the One who will one day receive you with the words, "Well done, good and faithful servant"

In the next and final section of this book, we will explore the greatest of all Bible mysteries—the mystery of our salvation!

Part V

THE MYSTERY OF OUR SALVATION

Whereby, when ye read, ye may understand my knowledge in the mystery of Christ.

Ephesians 3:4

"I do not wish to make a mystery," said he, laughing. "The matter was perfectly simple."
Sir Arthur Conan Doyle
"A Scandal in Bohemia"

HOW CAN A LOVING GOD
SEND PEOPLE TO HELL?

Billy Dukenfield's childhood was marked by pain and sadness. The son of a violent, hard-drinking saloon keeper and a chronically bitter, unhappy mother, young Billy grew up in the mean streets of inner-city Philadelphia in the 1880s. His home was a tiny apartment over the bar. His father beat him often, and Billy disliked and feared the man, but he was devoted to his mother.

Young Billy had one consolation in life: Christmastime. Though the presents he received were meager and usually secondhand, there was something about the carols and the celebration of the birth of the Christ child that seemed to soften his father's violent moods and brighten his mother's disposition.

But Billy's love of Christmas was shattered when he was only eight years old. As a grown man he recalled, "I had saved up some money carrying ice in Philadelphia, and I was going to buy my mother a copper-bottomed clothes boiler for Christmas. I hid the money in a brown crock in the coal bin, but my father found the crock. He stole the money and got drunk. Ever since then, I've remembered nobody on Christmas, and I want nobody to remember me."

The embittered boy ran away from home when he was only eleven. He supported himself with various odd jobs and learned to juggle and tell jokes by watching circus and vaudeville performers. By the age of nineteen, he was performing on the vaudeville stage himself. In the laughter and applause of the audiences, he found a substitute for the love he had lacked as a boy.

For years, he wouldn't touch a drop of liquor, not wanting to become anything like his hated father. He would buy drinks for his friends, but would never touch the stuff himself. Unfortunately, drunks don't like to see a friend not drinking, so Billy's pals coaxed him into taking his first drink—which led to a second and a third and on and on. Before long, Billy acquired a quart-a-day whiskey habit.

As a young man, Billy Dukenfield had no use for God, and he lived his life as an agnostic. He became a successful star of film, stage, and radio. But the world knew him not by his given name, William Claude Dukenfield, but by his stage name, W. C. Fields—the comedic star of such films as *Never Give a Sucker an Even Break* and *My Little Chickadee*.

To this day, TV audiences still howl at his classic performances as a lovable, foggy, inebriated curmudgeon with an unintentional gift for stirring up trouble. Among his oft-quoted lines is the statement, "Anyone who hates dogs and children can't be all bad." But even today, few people know of the childhood pain and the tortured soul behind the laughter.

In the closing days of his life, W. C. Fields lay in a hospital bed facing the final reality that comes to us all. Ironically, this man who had hated Christmas since he was eight years old would die on Christmas Day, 1946—a wealthy, famous, but lonely man. Shortly before his death, one of his Hollywood friends stopped by the hospital to visit Fields. This friend was well acquainted with Fields's disdain for God, religion, and morality. So the man was shocked to find Fields sitting up in bed reading a Bible.

"Bill!" said the astonished friend. "What on earth are you doing?"

"Just looking for a loophole," was Fields's wry reply, "looking for a loophole."[1]

It seems to me that many people today are looking for loopholes. They seek some way to escape the deserved consequences of their sin.

Here, then, is the next Bible mystery we will explore: How can a loving God send anyone to Hell? Isn't there a contradiction between a God who punishes and a God of love?

A SECOND CHANCE AT SALVATION?

Some try to deny that there is a God who could possibly punish sin. Others try to deny that there is a hell where sin is punished. Still others try to deny that a loving God would ever send anyone to Hell—even such reprobates as themselves. One of the most common responses of agnostics and scoffers is to justify themselves by condemning God. "If there is a God," they say, "then He must be unjust and unfair and unloving. No loving God could ever send anyone to Hell." By slandering God in this way, they think they have proved that they are justified in rejecting Him and living their lives as they please.

Does God have to give everybody a chance to be saved? Must God extend mercy to everyone? Let me answer that question with a couple of questions of my own:

1. Have you ever given money to a beggar? If your answer is yes, then God bless you. You have shown mercy.
2. Have you given money to every beggar you ever met in your entire life?

Whenever I ask these two questions of an audience, many hands go up in response to the first question—but few, if any, hands go up at the second question. If you are like most people, your mercy is a bit selective. You give to some beggars and withhold from others.

So I have to ask you: How dare you! What do you mean by not giving money to *every* beggar you have ever seen? Who do you think you are? Why, you would think it was your own money you were giving away!

What's that you say? Oh, it *is* your own money? You worked for it and earned it? But what about the beggar? Isn't he entitled to some of your money? Aren't you morally required to give your money away to every beggar you meet on the street? No?

Well, isn't that interesting. Some people make the claim that God is morally required to show mercy to every human being on the planet. Why, then, are you not morally required to show mercy to every beggar on the planet?

Perhaps it is becoming clear that God owes mercy to no one. But in case you still doubt, let's look at another example. Suppose the president of the United States decides to use his presidential power to pardon a criminal. If he pardons one criminal, doesn't that mean he is morally obligated to pardon *every* criminal? If he pardons one, don't you think the people of this nation will rise up and demand that the doors of all the prisons be opened and every cell be emptied? Of course not.

No one is entitled to mercy. The God of all the earth "must do rightly," but He doesn't have to extend mercy to anyone. "I will have mercy on whom I will have mercy," says God in Romans 9:15, "and I will have compassion on whom I will have compassion." If mercy were earned or deserved by everyone, then it wouldn't be mercy; it would be justice. We all have a claim on justice, but no one has a claim on mercy. So it is simply not true that God must extend mercy to everyone.

My friend, God is not only loving and gracious, but He is also just and holy. Eternity is real. Hell is real. This is not a subject that I or anyone else likes to dwell on, but Christ, the loving Savior, is the One who declares it more frequently than anyone else in the Bible. We do not talk of Hell because we take some twisted pleasure in thoughts of death, punishment, or eternal suffering. No, we talk of Hell to *warn* people and *spare* them such a fate. Our loving Savior has given Himself for our sins so that we don't have to pay the awful price ourselves. He took Hell onto Himself when He hung upon the cross.

Remember the night before the crucifixion? Jesus went to the Garden of Gethsemane to pray. There, unseen by any other eyes, a cup appeared before him—a symbolic cup, but what it represented was very real. It was a representation of all the world's sin—every lie, every murder, every hateful word, every lustful thought, every adultery, every fornication, every perverted act, every broken promise. All of our sins, too numerous to imagine, were distilled into that cup.

And Jesus looked into that cup, and His holy mind and soul recoiled from what He saw. We who swim in a sea of sin have been desensitized to the true awfulness of it. But Jesus, who knew no sin, recoiled in horror at the sight of it, and He implored the Father, "O my Father, if it be possible, let this cup pass from me." And for an hour He prayed, then He returned to find His disciples sleeping. As He faced the most awesome choice in human history, they slept. So He went back and prayed again for another hour. "O, my Father, if it be possible, let this cup pass from me." And again, the third time, after which He said, "Nevertheless not as I will, but as thou wilt" (Matt. 26:39).

The next day, impaled upon the Cross, lifted up naked before the world, He endured the shame and agony not only of the Cross, but of that cup. He spent the last three interminable hours of His life upon that Cross, until high noon. Then the sun's light failed, and noonday turned to midnight. And there in that darkness, unseen by mortal eyes, the hand of God reached out from Heaven and put that vile cup to His lips, and He drank it to the dregs. At that moment, Jesus Christ, the Holy One of God, *became sin* for us.

Then His Father, who loved the Son with an infinite and eternal love, turned over the cauldron of His wrath, and poured it out upon Jesus. Yes, God also loves you and me with an infinite love—but He hates sin with an infinite hate. So His wrath spilled out upon His own Son, washing over Him like the fires of Hell. And, at last, when it seemed an eternity had passed, Jesus cried, "It is finished. *Tetelestai*—the debt is paid in full."

God has sworn that He will punish our sins. If they are not punished, God becomes a liar. So He will either punish them on us—or He will punish them upon His Son. The choice is yours to make.

There, my friend, is the loophole that the dying comedian was searching for as he thumbed through his Bible on his deathbed. I hope he found it.

Have you found that loophole? Jesus created it out of His own agony and anguish upon the Cross. He created it by drinking the cup of God's wrath—a cup that was poured for you, and which, by all that is just, should have been yours to drink. Instead, He offers you the cup of His mercy and eternal life. Have you accepted it?

JUSTICE AND MERCY

A middle-aged woman went to a portrait photographer to have her picture taken. Sometime later, she picked up the portrait and brought it home. She was obviously displeased with the photo. "Look at this!" she declared, showing it to her husband. "This picture doesn't do me justice!"

"Dear," her husband replied, "what you need is not justice, but mercy."

Seconds later, *he* needed mercy!

We all need mercy, don't we? And thanks be to God, He has extended to us mercy upon mercy through His Son, Jesus. Justice and law came through Moses, but grace and truth and the mercy of God came through Jesus Christ. Many people have difficulty understanding the Christian faith because it is so different from what they would expect if they had written the Bible. Most people, if they were making up the Christian religion themselves, would do away with mercy altogether. They would set up the rules in this way:

Rule 1: The good people go to Heaven.
Rule 2: The bad people go to Hell.

In fact, many people who have never really taken a close look at Christianity think that is how it actually works. It sounds like a good idea. It sounds fair. And it's so simple. We could just get rid of all those lengthy books of the Old and New Testaments, and simply substitute those two simple rules.

But that is not how Christianity works at all. Why? Because if that were the way Christianity worked, Heaven would be an empty place. There is a problem with those two simple rules: *There aren't any good people!*

We don't like to hear that. We like to think of ourselves as good people. But the Bible doesn't leave that illusion to us. It tells us, "They are altogether become filthy; there is none that doeth good, no, not one" (Ps. 53:3). "For there is not a just man upon earth, that doeth good, and sinneth not" (Eccles. 7:20). "As it is written, There is none righteous, no, not one; . . . They are together become unprofitable" (Rom. 3:10, 12).

So we have a very serious problem on our hands. We are all sinners. Our problem cannot be solved with justice or fairness—for justice *is* the problem! We *deserve* punishment—we have earned it with our sin. Justice only places us under condemnation. We need mercy, not justice.

I once had a conversation with a flight attendant, who said she had a difficult time accepting the Christian faith. "Christianity just isn't fair," she said. "It's not fair that just a tiny group of people are saved. Meanwhile, there are all these other people who deserve to be saved as much as the ones who are saved, but they are eternally lost. That's just not fair."

"Well," I said, "let's take a look at that. That tiny group of people you mention is approximately two billion strong. It is the largest religion by far on this planet and almost twice the size of its closest competitor. And secondly, Christianity cordially invites all the people of the world to come, and promises that they will never be turned away." And I proceeded to explain to her the plan of salvation by grace through faith in Jesus Christ.

"But it's still not fair," the woman insisted, shaking her head. "The way it should be is that if you do good, you go to Heaven. If you do bad, you go to Hell. But being saved by grace—well, it's just not fair."

"You're exactly right," I agreed. "Now you've got it. Christianity is not fair. God is not fair. The Bible is not fair. Salvation is not fair. And that's the beauty of it. If everything were fair, no one would go to Heaven—everyone would go to Hell."

I wish I could report that this flight attendant made a decision for Christ on that airplane, but she did not. She could not get past the idea that salvation should be "fair." Somehow, she could not grasp the fact that Christianity is far *better* than fair.

Let me give you an example to explain the point. Let's say you have a ten-dollar bill and you take it to the bank and ask to have it changed for one-dollar bills. You take it to the teller's window and the teller counts out ten one-dollar bills. That's just; that's fair.

But what if the teller gave you *seven* one-dollar bills in exchange for your ten-dollar bill? You'd say, "That's not fair!" You would feel cheated.

Now suppose the teller gave you seven *thousand-dollar* bills for your ten? Well, that's not fair, is it? But I doubt you would complain!

And that's what God's grace and mercy are like. That's what salvation is like. It's not fair, true. But is it *below* fair? Is it a cheat, like getting seven ones for a ten-dollar bill? No! It is unfair because it is *above* and *beyond* fair!

Salvation is by grace, and grace is a unique concept among all the world religions. Grace just doesn't exist in any other religion. All other religions operate on some version of justice and fairness—if you simply do good works, you can go to Heaven. But Christianity stands in stark contrast to all other justice-oriented religions. Christianity says there is no one who does good. There is no one who gets to Heaven by good works. The only people in Heaven will be sinners like you and me. Heaven will be completely populated by the undeserving. Everyone in Heaven will be there because salvation is not fair.

And thank God, it's not fair! Salvation is gracious. Heaven is a mercy. That is what Christianity is all about. Grace and mercy are the antithesis of justice and fairness. And against that, you and I have no complaint.

WHAT IS GRACE?

Over the years, I have noticed that unless a person has been transformed by grace, and changed by Christ, that person doesn't really know what grace is. If you haven't experienced grace, you can't define it or explain it. Now, that is remarkable. Most people can explain many things without ever having experienced them. You may never have had a heart attack, but most people have at least an approximate idea of what a heart attack is. But if you ask a non-Christian, "What is God's grace?" you will probably get a blank stare and a shrug.

Even Christians are sometimes surprisingly vague about the meaning of grace. I have heard some of them say, "Well, grace is when God goes easy on us. He sort of grades on a curve and lets some people into heaven even though they're not perfect." Sorry! Wrong answer! God definitely does *not* grade on a curve! His standard is absolute perfection, as Jesus explained in Matthew 5:48—"Be ye therefore perfect, even as your Father which is in heaven is perfect." So if you want to be good enough to go to Heaven, the rule is very simple and plain: All you have to do is live an entire lifetime without committing one sin. Do that, and you will not be turned away.

What's that? You say you've *already* sinned? Well, how many times? You mean you've sinned so many times you can't even count them all? Well, that's too bad! It seems you are out of luck, because God's justice demands nothing less than perfection.

But as we've already discussed, a standard of sinless perfection would make a ghost town of Heaven—and I'm sure God didn't create Heaven just to let it stand vacant. So that brings us back to grace. Clearly, grace is not just a matter of God "grading on a curve." There is something much deeper and richer and more profound to the grace of God than that.

Someone has suggested an acrostic that fittingly describes grace:

<u>G</u>od's
<u>R</u>iches
<u>A</u>t
<u>C</u>hrist's
<u>E</u>xpense

What are God's riches? Forgiveness, pardon, eternal life, paradise forever and ever. What was Christ's expense? The scourging, the spikes in His hands and feet, the cross, the agony, the blood, the cup of all our sin and all God's wrath poured out upon Him. That is what GRACE is.

You may be thinking, *I can never receive His grace. My sins are too great. I'm beyond the reach of His forgiveness.* My friend, Christ was crucified next to a thief, and He said to the dying criminal, "Today shalt thou be with me in paradise" (Luke 23:43). The sea of God's grace is always deeper than the deepest sins. Cast a mountain of sin into that sea, and the depths of God's grace will not even begin to be sounded. Like the Flood in Noah's day, His grace will cover entire continents and mountain ranges of sin. Your sins will be buried in the depths of that sea, to be remembered against you no more.

You may think the enormity of your sin will bar you from receiving God's grace. But no, the awareness and horror of your sin is actually *preparing* you to receive His grace. It is not horrible sinners who are beyond God's grace and acceptance. Instead, it is the people who insist, "I'm a good person, I've led a good life," who are actually furthest from His grace. No one is good. No one is acceptable to God.

There may be a person sitting next to you who has committed one-tenth as many sins as you. And there may be another person nearby who has committed ten times as many sins as you. None of that matters, because God's standard is perfection, and everyone falls short of that standard. There is none who is good, no, not one. So the ground is level at the foot of the Cross.

You may think you are a good person compared to the people around you. And you may even be right. But all that means is that you will be one of the better people in Hell!

If you would rather be a sinner in Heaven by the grace of God than one of the better people in Hell, then you need to recognize the fact that you are a sinner. If you can't admit you are a sinner, then you cannot receive grace. God's grace works for no one but sinners.

IS JESUS THE ONLY WAY TO GOD?

People often ask, "Is Jesus the only way to God?" Answering yes to that question flies in the face of our cultural climate. The dominant virtue of this secular, pluralistic age is, of course, "tolerance." Most people today believe that the many religions in the world are merely different roads leading to the same destination. To say that there is only one road to God and that all the rest lead into a wilderness or a dead end is to be hopelessly intolerant!

I am often accused of such intolerance. When that accusation arises, I respond, "Are you referring to *true* tolerance or the *new* tolerance?" Since the inception of the English language, the word *tolerance* has always meant the quality of putting up with views with which you don't agree, and doing it in a kind and courteous fashion. That is true tolerance.

But when people speak of tolerance today, that is not what they mean. The new tolerance is a "politically correct" tolerance (and I put "politically correct" in quotation marks because, of course, there is nothing more truly incorrect than so-called "political correctness"!). This new tolerance means that you not only must be kind and courteous, but you must treat all ideas as equally valid and true. So if someone says, "I believe the way to God is by meditating with crystals in each hand," or "I believe the way to God is through drugs such as LSD," then we Christians must affirm those views as every bit the equal of the Christian view.

According to the new tolerance, we must no longer quote the "intolerant" words of Jesus in John 14:6: "I am the way, the truth, and the life: no man cometh unto the Father, but by me." Those words are not inclusive. They might offend the Buddhist, the Muslim, the Scientologist, the agnostic. According to the new tolerance, all intellectual viewpoints are equally valid, equally true. You have your truth. I have my truth. But there is no such thing as *true* truth.

The fact is, not all points of view are equal. What is true for me is true for you and true for every other person on the planet. People may wander around in a haze of subjective opinion and irrational belief, but that does not change the fact that the universe is founded upon objective truth, true truth.

Two men are crossing a road. One looks up and shouts, "Hey! There's a truck coming around the corner! If we don't hurry, we'll be killed!" And he proceeds to run off the road.

But the other man stays in the middle of the road. "A truck, you say? That may be true for you, but it's not true for—"

Splat!

Famous last words! And what is true of that man in the street is even more true of the men and women around us who are blindly sauntering toward eternity, unaware of the everlasting fate that is bearing down on their souls.

The idea that there is no objective truth is called *relativism.* All things are relative, they say. Oh, really? So 2 + 2 does not always equal 4? Sometimes it equals 3 or 5 or even 372, depending on our belief system? Would you want to be treated by a doctor who says that it's all relative, all a matter of personal opinion, how much of a certain drug he puts in the hypodermic syringe he is preparing to plunge into your arm? Would you want to cross a bridge that was built by someone who believes in engineering relativism? Would you want to fly in an airplane built by someone who believes that the laws of aerodynamics are all relative, a matter of personal preference?

I wouldn't. I trust true truth, and I trust other people who believe in true truth. All viewpoints are *not* equal.

Jesus made a monumental declaration when He said, "I am the way, the truth, and the life: no man cometh unto the Father, but by me" (John 14:6). He made it clear, in certain and unambiguous terms: Jesus Christ is not one of many ways to Heaven, as people often claim. He is either the only way to God, or He is no way to God at all. He is either the truth, or He is a lie. He is either the life, or He is a fraud whose bones are still buried in a tomb in Palestine.

So if someone attempts to patronize you by saying, "I'm glad you're so sincere about Jesus. I, too, believe He is a way to God, one of many ways to God," you can say, "No, thank you. Please do not patronize me, and do not patronize Christ. He cannot be one of many ways to God. If you do not accept Him as *the* Way, *the* Truth, and *the* Life, please do Him the courtesy of simply, honestly rejecting Him."

Yes, I know that's an intolerant thing to say. The truth usually is.

Understand that when Jesus declares Himself to be the only way to God, He is not alone in this view. This is not some statement of His that I have wrenched out of context and twisted to suit my own purposes. This is the consistent, pervasive view of *all* of Scripture. The apostle Paul said, "For there is one God, and one mediator between God and men, the man Christ Jesus" (1 Tim. 2:5). And Peter, boldly addressing the Sanhedrin in Jerusalem, said: "Neither is there salvation in any other: for there is none other name under heaven given among men, whereby we must be saved" than the name of Jesus Christ (Acts 4:12).

Some might say, "Well, that is a provincial and narrow viewpoint, reflecting the views of an ancient culture that is not as enlightened and inclusive and pluralistic as our own." But the truth is that Christianity arose in the first century at a crossroads of many different cultures and languages and religions. It arose and spread like wildfire through the most cosmopolitan and pluralistic cities this world has ever known—in such places as Jerusalem, Antioch, Athens, Corinth, and Rome. The early Christians did not embrace this faith because they were so backward and exposed to so few new ideas. They were surrounded and bombarded by ideas and philosophies and religions all the time—but only one faith had the ring of truth, the ring of reality. Only one faith offered a Person who was the Way, the Truth, and the Life. The early Christians had all belonged to other religions at one time, but they had converted to Jesus Christ because He had the words of eternal life.

The first book ever written against Christianity was written by an arch-heretic named Celsus. "It makes no difference," he wrote, "if one invokes the highest God or Zeus or Adonai or Sabaoth or Amoun, as the Egyptians do, or Papaios, as the Scythians do." He penned those words during the second century A.D., proving that little has changed in nearly two thousand years. We live in a pluralistic society today that says all roads lead to God, and Celsus expressed the very same sentiments in that ancient era. We have always lived in a pluralistic world. But then and now, there is only one Way, one Truth, one Life.

People have sometimes asked me, "Are you telling me that Christianity is the only way to Heaven?"

My answer often surprises them. "No," I say, "it is not."

Usually, their mouths drop open in amazement.

"Christianity," I continue, "is not the way to Heaven at all. Jesus never said that it is. Neither did Peter or Paul. Christianity is not the way. *Christ* is the way. 'I am the way, the truth, and the life,' He said. 'No man cometh unto the Father, but by me.' The way to Heaven is not a religion. It's a Person."

All of the religions in the world have a way. In fact, Taoism is a religious philosophy that actually means "The Way." Every religion says, "Here is the way; walk ye in it." But Jesus did not say that. He did not reveal the way. He did not point the way. He did not lead the way. He said, "*I am* the way."

The way is His incarnate body broken for us. The Way is His blood of infinite value, shed for our sins. The Way is His Resurrection that saves and redeems mankind, the promise of the new life for us all.

Rituals, tithes, piety, prayers, sacraments, traditions—none of these things can save. Only Jesus saves. When He hung upon the Cross, He hung alone. When He drank the cup of our sin, the cup of God's wrath, He drank it alone. Buddha, Muhammad, Confucius—none of them could even share the cup with Him. None of them could sip a single drop. The Father gave it to Jesus alone, the sinless One, and He drank all of it for you and me. No one else even offered to share that cup, to endure that wrath with Christ.

Are there many roads to God? Are there many roads to Heaven? If there are, then Jesus died for nothing. If it is possible to be saved apart from Jesus Christ, then He needn't have died on the cross. His suffering was wasted.

But we know that Jesus did *not* die for nothing. He died for your sins and mine, for the sins of the world. And we know, beyond the faintest shadow of a doubt, that "there is none other name under heaven given among men, whereby we must be saved" (Acts 4:12).

WHAT ABOUT THOSE WHO HAVE NEVER HEARD?

Throughout this chapter, we have been looking at various issues surrounding the Bible mystery of God's judgment. Now we come to a corollary question that troubles many people, both Christians and non-Christians: What about those who have never heard the Gospel? How can God send people who have never even heard of Christ to Hell? How can that be fair and just?

Skeptics and scoffers often state this question in an abrasive and irate fashion: "Do you mean to tell me that God would condemn people to Hell simply for not believing in a Savior they never heard of? What kind of monstrous God would do that?" I call this *the ignorance defense*: How could God condemn someone for mere ignorance?

In our own legal system there is a principle that states, "Ignorance of the law is no excuse." But, in fact, God is not as harsh and ruthless as our legal system. God is not a monster. God is love. And God does, in fact, take ignorance into consideration. It is we humans who don't. It is we who are the monsters, with our harsh and unforgiving legal system, so let's get the story straight.

When we think of ignorance, when we imagine people who have never heard the Gospel of Jesus Christ, we usually think (in stereotypical terms) of people in the midst of "darkest Africa" or India or China. But we forget that we have a great deal of ignorance of the Gospel right here in America, especially since we banished God from our public school classrooms a few decades ago. As a result, we have produced an entire generation of people who are almost completely biblically illiterate. For example, these are actual statements that were written by American young people:

- In the first book of the Bible, Guinnesses, God got tired of creating and took the Sabbath off.
- Adam and Eve were created from an apple tree.
- Noah's wife was called Joan of Ark.
- Samson slayed the Philistines with the axe of the Apostles.
- The Egyptians were all drowned in the dessert. Afterwards, Moses went up on Mount Cyanide and got the Ten Amendments.
- The first commandment was when Eve told Adam to eat the apple.
- Moses died before he ever reached Canada. Then Joshua led the Hebrews in the battle of Geritol.
- Solomon had 300 wives and 700 porcupines.
- The people who followed the Lord were the 12 decibels.
- The epistles were the wives of the apostles.
- And the greatest miracle in all of the Bible is when Joshua told his son to stand still and he did.

Well, that would indeed be humorous if it wasn't so tragic. The ignorance you might expect to find in the farthest corners of the world is really right around the corner from your door.

Now, the ignorance defense proposed by the skeptics and scoffers presupposes that those who have never heard the Gospel are *completely* ignorant—*utterly* and *hopelessly* ignorant of God. Therefore, it would be a crime to condemn them for the fact that they simply haven't heard the Gospel. But let's question that presupposition for a moment. Is anyone, regardless of where and when he or she lives, *completely* ignorant of God?

God has revealed Himself to all mankind in at least one of three ways:

1. the light of creation

2. the light of conscience

3. the light of Christ

THE LIGHT OF CREATION

Because that which may be known of God is manifest in them; for God hath shewed it unto them. For the invisible things of him from the creation of the world are clearly seen, being understood by the things that are made, even his eternal power and Godhead; so that *they are without excuse:* Because that, when they knew God, they glorified him not as God, neither were thankful; but became vain in their imaginations, and their foolish heart was darkened. Professing themselves to be wise, they became fools. (Rom. 1:19–22, emphasis added)

What's more, this principle is an ancient one, first set forth in the Old Testament. There, the psalmist states that God has revealed Himself to all mankind in the light of creation: "The heavens declare the glory of God; and the firmament sheweth his handywork" (Ps.19:1).

All around the world, whenever people look up at the night sky and see the vast spray of stars scattered like diamond dust on black velvet, they realize that the universe was created by a Mind much greater than our own. As the hymn writer said, "The hand that made us is divine,"[2] and so it is. All over the world, people have come to believe in God simply by gazing awestruck at creation—unless their thinking has been distorted by some clever philosophy of atheism or unbelief.

Even in America, where generations of children have been processed through atheistic state-run schools bent on destroying their faith, the most recent studies continue to show that some 95 percent of Americans believe in God. They have the light of creation to proclaim that God really does exist. So they are not ignorant of God.

THE LIGHT OF CONSCIENCE

The creation itself is the first source of light that shatters the ignorance defense. And there is a second source of light that God has given to humanity. It is described in Romans 2—the light of conscience. In the conscience, God judges the secrets of human beings. The conscience is where their thoughts either accuse or excuse them. God has placed a moral monitor in the hearts of men and women so that they know that some things are right and other things are wrong.

Now, the conscience can be slowly seared, as with a hot iron, by repeated violations, but it is never completely gone. Even when the conscience is dulled by being seared, people are accountable for the choices they have made that have produced a seared conscience. The evidence for the conscience of humanity is quite plain, as Paul explained in Romans 2:1–3:

> Therefore thou art inexcusable, O man, whosoever thou art that judgest: for wherein thou judgest another, thou condemnest thyself; for thou that judgest doest the same things. But we are sure that the judgment of God is according to truth against them which commit such things. And thinkest thou this, O man, that judgest them which do such things, and doest the same, that thou shalt escape the judgment of God?

Let's say that a man lives in a part of the world where the Gospel has never penetrated. One day he comes home to his hut and says to his wife, "Do you know what our neighbor in the next hut did to me? He lied to me! He's just no good! I'll never speak to that low-down liar again!"

Years later this man dies and comes before the judgment of God, and God lists the sins he has committed in his life. And somewhere in that list, God says, "You are guilty of lying."

"Me? Guilty of lying?" the man replies. "You can't hold me accountable for that! I didn't know it was wrong to lie! I never even heard of the Ten Commandments until I got to this place! You can't condemn me for doing something I didn't even know was wrong!"

So God leans over to one of His angels and says, "Would you play that tape back, please?"

And we travel back across the years and hear him storming into his hut and complaining to his wife. "Do you know what our neighbor in the next hut did to me?" says the man's voice from the tape. "He lied to me! He's just no good! I'll never speak to that low-down liar again!"

"Now," says God, "you were about to tell me that you didn't know that it is wrong to lie?"

And though he has never heard the Gospel, has never even heard of the Ten Commandments, he stands without excuse before God. He cannot claim ignorance, because he has already judged others guilty of the same sin of which he tried to excuse himself. If a man judges others but commits the same sins, how can he escape the judgment of God? The witness of conscience is very clear. God has given that much light to every single person who has ever lived on this earth.

If anyone would simply worship the true God and Creator who so clearly manifests Himself in the starry night and the grandeur of the mountains and the oceans and the skies, and if that person would simply live according to the dictates of his own conscience, then that person would enter into Heaven. Now, I hasten to add that no such person has yet applied at the gates of Heaven, but if he did, he would be welcomed by angel choirs.

Why has no such person applied at the gates? Because every human being who has ever lived is guilty of violating whatever light God may have given him. Therefore, he is without excuse. He cannot claim the ignorance defense, because he knows full well that he has done wrong.

I have traveled over most of this world and have talked to people from every continent. I have asked this question of people from all cultural and religious backgrounds and of people without any religion whatsoever: "Have you ever done anything that you believed was wrong?" Invariably, the answer comes back: "Are you kidding? Of course I have!" Every human being is without excuse. All have sinned, and all know it full well.

The light of creation and the light of conscience are given to everyone on earth. God will be just; He cannot be unjust. We all stand guilty before God, and His justice is justice indeed. The ignorance defense will not work, because we simply are not ignorant.

Now, God does take into consideration precisely *how much* we know and do not know. Of those who have received much light, much will be required, as the Scriptures say (Luke 12:48). We will not be judged about what we don't know; we will be judged about what we *do* know. As someone once said, "It's not what I *don't* know about the Bible that bothers me, it's what I *do* know!" God holds us accountable for what we know. The Judge of all the earth must do rightly—and that is our problem.

THE LIGHT OF CHRIST

Now, there is a *third* light that not all of the world has received, and it is described in Romans 3. It is not the light of creation, nor the light of conscience, but the light of Christ. It is the light of the grace and mercy of Jesus Christ, who came into this world to take all of our guilt, all of our sins upon Himself, and to endure the outpouring of God's wrath that we ourselves deserve. That is the light of Christ, the light of grace, and it is not incumbent upon God to extend it to anyone. Grace is not *owed* to anyone, or it would not be grace—it would be a debt.

If some hear the Gospel of Christ and others do not, does that mean that God is unfair? No. The Gospel is inclusive. No one is kept outside God's kingdom because of race or social status or education or income. All are invited to come and receive mercy.

Yes, some will hear the Gospel, and others will die without hearing.

But that does not mean that those who did not hear the Gospel have been unfairly treated. It only means that those who did hear were granted mercy. God does not owe mercy to anyone—only justice.

If God owed mercy to everyone who had not heard the Gospel, then all you would need for admission to heaven is ignorance of the Gospel! In that case, ignorance truly *would* be a defense. In that case, the worst thing you could do to a person is share the Gospel with him, because then you would remove his ignorance and imperil his soul! In that case, you would have to say that the human race had its best opportunity for salvation *before* Christ was born, because before Christ, the whole world was blissfully on its ignorant way to Heaven. But then Jesus came into the world, began preaching the Gospel, and suddenly people lost their ignorance, became responsible for what they had heard—and souls started descending into Hell by the dozens, the hundreds, and ultimately the millions.

If God owed mercy to those who had never heard the Gospel, then the world would be a better place if Jesus had never been born. We would have to stop celebrating Christmas and begin mourning the day He ever showed up on the planet. In that case, Jesus entered a world that was saved by its ignorance, and He only succeeded in condemning millions to Hell!

What's more, every Christian who helps spread the Gospel is doing nothing but ruining lives and condemning souls. The Evangelism Explosion program for training lay witnesses, a program that began at our church and has spread worldwide, would be doing the world a monstrous disservice. If God owed mercy to those who never heard the Gospel, it would be far better to have an evangelism *implosion* than an *explosion*. It would be far better to fire all the preachers, close all the churches, burn all the Bibles, and leave everyone in his or her ignorance. That is what happens when we take the ignorance defense to its logical conclusion: total chaos and absurdity.

But that is not the way the world works, my friend. When Jesus came, the world lay in darkness, under the heavy yoke of the devil. All of mankind was lost in sin until the glad tidings came, and the angel proclaimed that a Savior was born in Bethlehem. Ignorance of that truth is not bliss—and it is no defense against the righteous judgment of God.

Jesus Christ told us how the world works, and He told us what He expects us to do about it: "Go ye into all the world," He said, "and preach the gospel to every creature" (Mark 16:15). Those who believe shall be saved, and those that do not believe will be everlastingly condemned. And the responsibility rests with us.

There is a fictional story that makes a profound and truthful point. In this story, Christ has ascended to heaven following His resurrection. Arriving in Heaven, He gathers all the angels and archangels and tells them the story of His adventure on earth. He tells them about His birth in a stable, about the life that He has lived, about the people He taught and healed and raised from the dead. He tells them about His disciples and about the corrupt religious leaders who condemned Him. The angels begin to weep as He describes His agony on the Cross—the very agony of the damned.

Then He describes the Resurrection. He tells of appearing to His disciples and commissioning them to go and be His witnesses. He describes the Gospel message that He has entrusted to them—the message that those who place their trust in Him will not perish but have everlasting life.

But then one of the younger angels raises a hand to ask a question. "But these people You have commissioned as Your witnesses," the angel says. "They are human, aren't they?"

"Yes," says Jesus, "they are."

"They disobey and they rebel," the angel observes.

"Yes," answers Jesus, sighing, "they often have."

"So," says the angel, "what if they fail You? What if they don't do as You commanded? What if they don't go out and tell the world what You have done? What is Your backup plan?"

"I have no backup plan," says Christ.

And though this story is fiction, the point it makes is absolutely, devastatingly true. Jesus our Lord has no backup plan. He has entrusted the Gospel to you and to me. If we fail, there is no other plan.

So the question has been asked: How can a loving God allow anyone to go into a Christless eternity? But the real question should be: How can *we*? If we claim to be Christians, obedient servants of the will of Christ, then how can *we* allow anyone to go into eternity without hearing the Gospel of Jesus Christ?

God, in His infinite mercy, has already done all that He could. He has paid for the sins of the world at the infinite cost of His own Son's blood. What more could He do than that?

Now the world must be told. The Gospel must be shared.

And that responsibility rests with us. If we don't tell others, who really is unloving, God or man?

Mystery 13

ARE WE SAVED
BY FAITH OR WORKS?

T here are 40,000 varieties of religion on this planet. In this chapter I
will explain each of them to you. What's that? You don't believe I
can explain all 40,000 religions in a single chapter?

Well, I assure you I can. You see, all 40,000 of these religions really
boil down to three essential forms. It is not surprising that people consider religion such an incredibly complicated subject that they cannot
make their way through the labyrinth of all the many belief systems.
But once you see that all of these individual systems actually fit into
three categories, it all becomes simple and comprehensible.

What is religion, after all? It is a system of believing and behaving
that human beings have devised in an attempt to become attuned and in
harmony with God. And the goal of becoming right with God through
religion is that human beings might obtain eternal life, happiness, bliss,
joy, and paradise. All religions are pointed toward these goals, even
though some religions, such as Buddhism, would define "God" as an
impersonal principle rather than a personal being. Even in religions
without a personal God, the goal is to attain harmony with the underly-
ing reality of the universe, which produces eternal felicity in the form of
nirvana or *satori* or some other variation of spiritual apotheosis.

The three ways in which religion seeks to achieve harmony with
God and eternal bliss are:

1. the way of works alone

2. the way of faith alone

3. the way of faith plus works

The first and third ways require an individual to accomplish salvation (either in whole or in part) by his or her own efforts. The second way, the way of faith alone, is a different matter entirely. It is the way of faith in Jesus Christ, and it is the only way to God that is entirely free. Some people point to Bible verses that indicated that salvation is completely free, received by faith alone. Others point to Bible passages that seem to suggest that we are saved, in part, by good works. What is the truth?

Come with me, my friend, and together we will solve this last and most important Bible mystery!

THE FIRST WAY: SALVATION BY WORKS

Let's begin by looking at the first way to God, the way of works. By far, most of the 40,000 different religious varieties would fall into this main classification—salvation by works. This kind of religion operates on the principle that human beings are justified (pardoned, accepted, forgiven, and received into everlasting bliss) by God on the basis of the things they have done and the lives they have lived.

This is the most common religious view. You hear it all the time: "I think God's going to receive me when I die—at least, I hope He will. I've tried to live a good life. I've been a pretty good person. I try to follow the Golden Rule and the Ten Commandments—well, most of them, anyway." This rationale takes various forms in other cultures or religious traditions: "I follow the eight-fold path of Buddha," or "I follow the teachings of Confucius," or "I follow the writings of Muhammad and the precepts of the Koran," or "I keep the Ten Commandments or the Golden Rule." Each of these religious approaches is a works-centered approach.

If I do enough good works, the reasoning goes, *then God [or what-ever substitutes for God in that religious system] will receive me and accept me into Heaven.* Even religions that have no Heaven, per se, still operate on this principle. In Hinduism, your works, both good and bad, attach to your soul in the form of a principle called *karma.* Your goal in life is to amass as much good karma as possible, which enables you to have a good rebirth (reincarnation) after you die. The ultimate goal of the Hindu is to escape the cycles of rebirth and achieve *nirvana,* a kind of blissful nothingness, and at the base of it all is a belief in the efficacy of good works.

A works-centered religion is ultimately a self-centered religion. The focus is on *what I must do to save myself.* Each person becomes his or her own savior. There is no grace, no faith, no peace and security in God. To embrace such a religion is to live your life on a treadmill, always striving and never knowing if you have done enough. There is no reliance upon God, only reliance upon self. If you are going to be saved, you must do it yourself. You must become your own savior.

Salvation by works is the view of *every pagan religion in the world.* But you don't have to go to some foreign land to find people who prac-tice this approach. It is very popular right here in America. In fact, sal-vation by works is actually practiced by many nominal Christians in churches across this land. Over my years in ministry, I have met liter-ally hundreds of people who base their hope of Heaven on the fact that they are decent people, that they do acts of kindness to others, that they give time and money to good causes, and so forth. It is laudable to be that kind of person, of course, but good works do not save you, according to the truth of God's Word.

Justification by works *seems* to make sense, but as the Scriptures tell us, "There is a way which *seemeth* right unto a man, but the end thereof are the ways of death" (Prov. 14:12, emphasis mine). Salvation by works *seems* right—but if you place your faith in your own works to save you, the end of it all will be your own eternal, spiritual death.

Salvation by works is probably the religious starting point of every person on this planet. I once held that view, before I was found by Christ. So, in all likelihood, did you. There was a time when your hope of eternal life was based upon your own goodness. It seems so logical and reasonable, and the reason it seems that way to the human mind is that there is "a way which seemeth right unto a man or a woman"—until that man or woman begins to grasp the reality of God's grace and the meaning of justification by faith. If you have never made that transition from salvation by works to salvation by grace through faith, then you are still on that broad road that leads to destruction. You are still following that old, man-made religion, the "way which seemeth right," but ends in death.

To trust your own good works for salvation is pure, unadulterated paganism. It has nothing to do with authentic Christianity.

THE SECOND WAY: SALVATION BY FAITH ALONE

The second way is the way of salvation by faith in Jesus Christ. In theology, the doctrine of salvation is called *soteriology*. It comes from the Greek words *soter*, which means "savior," and *ology*, "the study of." Notice the vast difference between salvation by faith in Christ alone versus salvation by works. It is the contrast between *soteriology* (salvation by faith in the Savior, Jesus Christ) versus *auto-soterism* (self-salvation—"I am saving myself; glory be to me!"). Faith in Christ is the very antithesis of salvation by good works.

The pagan way of looking at life and morality is to see life as a kind of ledger in which good deeds are recorded as assets and bad deeds are recorded as liabilities. If you have more good deeds than bad, goes this pagan line of reasoning, then you are morally and spiritually "in the black." If you have more bad deeds than good, you are "in the red."

But God is not some Cosmic Accountant, checking to see if your books balance, making sure that you show a net profit after the bad deeds are deducted from the good. No, God's standard is not that the ledger of your life be "in the black," but rather that it be whiter than snow. In other words, His standard is sinless perfection. Jesus said, "Be ye therefore perfect, even as your Father which is in heaven is perfect" (Matt. 5:48). No amount of good deeds can erase even one black mark of sin from the ledger. And, of course, we are all aware that we have many, many more black marks than that! Jeremiah 17:9–10 tells us that God does not just look upon our works, but He searches the heart, and He knows that the human heart is "deceitful above all things, and desperately wicked."

So if we have to do good in order to gain admission to Heaven, then we would have to conclude that, biblically speaking, no one will ever make it. The Bible is emphatic on this point: "There is none good but . . . God" (Mark 10:18). If you think you are a "good person" and qualify for heaven on your own good merit, then you are in for a big surprise on the day of the final judgment. God Himself declares that you are *not* good. If there is even one single stain of sin on the ledger of your life, your "good works" defense will evaporate in a heartbeat. You will be instantly convicted and sentenced without possibility of appeal.

Neuroscientists estimate that roughly 10,000 thoughts go through the human mind every day. In the course of a day, we speak thousands and thousands of words. Suppose I asked you to recall the thoughts you thought and the words you spoke on September 3, 1983, or July 13, 1991, or January 27, 2000—how many thoughts and words would you be able to recall? Unless one of those dates happened to be your birthday or your wedding day or the day you drove your car into the swimming pool, you probably could not come up with a single thought or word. It has well been said that "a clear conscience is usually the result of a poor memory."

But God remembers *everything*.

If God remembers every sin we have committed, then we are truly doomed, aren't we? We are powerless to erase our sins from His memory. We cannot lift ourselves out of the mire of our own sinful condition. Our situation is utterly hopeless—

Unless God Himself provides a solution.

And that is exactly what biblical Christian faith holds to be true. We are justified by faith in Jesus Christ alone. Paul gave his great summary of the Gospel in Romans 3, concluding with this statement in verse 28: "Therefore we conclude that a man is justified by faith without the deeds of the law." Or, as Paul added in Galatians 2:16:

> Knowing that a man is not justified by the works of the law, but by the faith of Jesus Christ, even we have believed in Jesus Christ, that we might be justified by the faith of Christ, and not by the works of the law: for by the works of the law shall no flesh be justified.

Note that in that one verse there are six separate phrases, six distinct statements and restatements of the fact that salvation is by faith and not by works. That is pretty emphatic, isn't it?

So we believe in salvation by the pure unmerited grace of God, which is received purely and solely by faith in Jesus Christ. Therefore, eternal life is a free gift. Though it is true that the wages of sin is death, the gift of God is eternal life.

This is the view of all authentic Christianity: Salvation is by faith in Christ only. It is a free gift from God!

THE THIRD WAY:
SALVATION BY FAITH *PLUS* WORKS

The third view is held by most cults and by Roman Catholicism. This view combines the other two views, saying that we are saved by faith in Christ *plus* our good works. This view says that salvation is the result of what Christ did plus what I do. It is as if Jesus comes down and together He and I establish a Salvation Corporation, a partnership designed to save me. So He gets some of the glory and I get some of the glory. Did you spot the flaw in that scenario? It is a glaring one! The fact is that Jesus Christ will not share His glory with another. He is the

Lord. And everything that needs to be done to secure our salvation, He already accomplished on the Cross.

Those who believe in salvation by faith plus works invariably appeal to one Bible passage, James 2, for support. The reason they appeal to this text and no other is because it is the *only* place in the Bible that seems to support this view (properly interpreted, it does not). The rest of the Bible flatly contradicts this view. Whenever I have preached on James 2, there are always a number of people who come to me after the service and say, "I'm so glad I heard that message. That was the first time I've ever understood what James meant when he wrote that passage." In James 2:14, 18–20, we read:

> What doth it profit, my brethren, though a man say he hath faith, and have not works? can faith save him? If a brother or sister be naked, and destitute of daily food, and one of you say unto them, depart in peace, be ye warmed and filled; notwithstanding ye give them not those things which are needful to the body; what doth it profit? Even so faith, if it hath not works, is dead, being alone. Yea, a man may say, Thou hast faith, and I have works: shew me thy faith without thy works, and I will shew thee my faith by my works. Thou believest that there is one God; thou doest well: the devils also believe, and tremble. But wilt thou know, O vain man, that faith without works is dead?

Let's explore together what this passage is actually about. As we look at this passage together, I believe you will understand why the idea of salvation by faith plus works is just as mistaken and unbiblical as the idea of salvation by works alone. I would even encourage you to take your study Bible and mark it.

The secret of James 2 is found in what I call "the seven Ss" of James 2. I encourage you to mark each of those Ss in your Bible as we examine them. Draw a box around the word or use a yellow highlighting marker, as you wish. But mark the word *say* in verse 14 (I have marked it in bold italic):

What doth it profit, my brethren, though a man *say* he hath faith, and have not works? can faith save him?

Next, do the same thing in verses 16 and 18:

And one of you *say* unto them, Depart in peace, be ye warmed and filled; notwithstanding ye give them not those things which are needful to the body; what doth it profit? Yea, a man may *say*, Thou hast faith, and I have works: shew me thy faith without thy works, and I will shew thee my faith by my works.

Why is the word *say* so important in these passages? Because James used that word to make a very important distinction between the *claim* to faith and the *reality* of faith. Anyone can *say*, "I have faith in Christ." But the reality of such a claim can only be proved by a person's actions. If you say you have faith but live as an unbeliever, then your life proves that what you say is a lie. But if you live as one who believes in Christ, people will see your faith in your actions before you ever say a word.

Some people have said that there is a disagreement between Paul and James over faith versus works. They look at the passages of Paul that I cited earlier ("a man is justified by faith without the deeds of the law") and compare them with James 2 and they shout, "Fight! Fight!" But there is no fight between Paul and James, and there is no contradiction either. God's Word speaks with one voice, though written by many human writers, and the letters of Paul and James are no exception. If we started with the premise that all of Scripture speaks with a single voice, the voice of God, then we would not fall so easily into misunderstanding.

The misunderstanding over Paul and James involves a failure to grasp the different intentions of each writer. Paul dealt with the question, "How can I as an individual person be justified, pardoned, forgiven, and received by God?" Answer: By faith alone. But James was dealing with a different question: "How can I demonstrate the reality of my faith?" Answer: My faith will be evidenced through my works, through the way I live my life.

As Christians, we all have to deal with the issue that James raised. Whenever you profess to be a Christian, there will always be skeptics who deny the fact that God really lives within you. If you claim to be a Christian, someone will inevitably say, "Oh, yeah, you *say* you're a Christian, but you're going to have to prove it to me! I know what kind of life you've lived in the past. If your Christianity is real, then don't just talk about your faith. Show me! If your life doesn't show any difference, then why should I believe what you say?"

And that's just the point James made throughout this passage, and most particularly in verse 18: "Yea, a man may say, Thou hast faith, and I have works: shew me thy faith without thy works, and I will shew thee my faith by my works."

Paul is talking about our justification before God. James is talking about the justification of our profession of faith before men. Because I am in the public eye, in the pulpit, in print, and on radio and television, I am keenly aware of the point James was making. There is always someone who hates the Christian message and who will try to discredit my message by painting me as a hypocrite, as someone who professes one thing and lives another. I am continually aware of my need to live my life in such a way that others can see that my faith is real and genuine. And though you may not be in the public eye, the same is true of you and every other Christian: We must all demonstrate the reality of our faith by our works.

Before we leave James 2, there are several more *S*s I wish to bring to your attention. You see, faith is an invisible, intangible thing. The only way it can be made visible and tangible is through the way we live our lives. That is why the word *show* (or, in the King James Version, *shew*) appears so prominently in this text. It occurs twice in verse 18. (These are the fourth and fifth *S*s of the chapter.)

Yea, a man may say, Thou hast faith, and I have works: *shew* me thy faith without thy works, and I will *shew* thee my faith by my works.

I suggest you mark those two words in your Bible as I have emphasized them here. If your faith is real, *show* it to the world by the way you live your life and by the example you set.

In verses 22 and 24, we have a couple more Ss that I encourage you to mark in your Bible:

Seest thou how faith wrought with his works, and by works was faith made perfect? And the scripture was fulfilled which saith, Abraham believed God, and it was imputed unto him for righteousness: and he was called the Friend of God. Ye *see* then how that by works a man is justified, and not by faith only.

The key word in these verses is *see*. James was talking about a faith that is not just an inner belief, but a visible reality that the world can see. And the way that takes place is through our works, through the evidence of our lives. So the key words in these passages are the Ss— *say*, *show*, and *see*. We *say* that we are Christians, and every Christian professes that he is a believer, but belief is invisible. We must *show* it by the lives we live—and then the world will *see* the reality of it in our lives.

So, as we have demonstrated in our exploration of this passage, there is no conflict between one part of the Bible and another. If anyone is still not persuaded that James and Paul are in perfect harmony, then simply look back a few verses to James 2:10. There James said something that absolutely demolishes any suggestion that he was proposing salvation by faith plus works. There he wrote, "For whosoever shall keep the whole law, and yet offend in one point, he is guilty of all." There it is—God's standard of absolute perfection. Works are powerless to save, even if added to faith.

James understood as well as Paul that salvation is by grace through faith alone.

LEGALISM VERSUS LICENSE

One of my seminary professors, Dr. William Childs Robinson, used to say, "Christ always was and always will be crucified between two thieves—legalism and license." That is still going on today. Followers of Christ are under continual attack from these two sides. The legalists, like the Pharisees, are those that want to be justified before God by their works, by their law-keeping, by their scrupulous adherence to the fine points of the law. Paul, in many of his letters, had to fight against the legalists who would undermine the pure faith of the Church. So he continually pressed the point that we are not justified by the works of the law, but by faith in Jesus Christ.

James, however, found himself at odds with people from the other extreme, people who advocated license. Those people promoted a heresy called *antinomianism* (from the Greek *anti-* [against] and *nomos* [law]). The antinomians wanted to say, "I am saved by faith in Christ," yet live like pagans. They would come to church on Sunday, but Monday through Saturday, look out! They "talked the talk" but did not "walk the walk." James was battling this heresy in his epistle—and Paul, too, did battle against this same heresy in Romans 6, where he dealt with the question, "Shall we continue in sin, that grace may abound? God forbid. How shall we, that are dead to sin, live any longer therein?" (vv. 1–2). As A. W. Tozer once observed, "Antinomianism is the doctrine of grace carried by uncorrected logic to the point of absurdity. It takes the teaching of justification by faith and twists it into deformity."[1]

So Paul and James are totally in sync. It is as though these two great apostles stand back to back, swords in hand, battling attackers rushing them from both sides while defending the purity of faith in the middle. Together, they defend a single truth that both hold in common, that salvation is by grace through faith in Jesus Christ alone—and that the reality of that faith is demonstrated by the lives we live. Our works prove our faith, but they add nothing to the work of salvation that Jesus already accomplished on the Cross.

Imagine you are standing at the brink of a cliff. Across the chasm, 200 feet away, is another cliff. The distance to the bottom: 5,000 feet. You have to get across the chasm to the other side. You have a strong nylon rope that is capable of holding 3,000 pounds without breaking. It will easily support you—but it's only 100 feet long. You are 100 feet short of bridging the 200-foot gap.

Here I come to your rescue. "Don't worry," I say, "I was a Boy Scout. I'm always prepared. Here's a spool of thread—more than 100 feet long. We can tie my thread to your rope and you'll have no trouble getting across."

Would you trust your life to my spool of thread? Why not? It's very good thread. Oh, I see—you don't think it's strong enough to support you.

Well, let's change the scenario a bit. Let's say that instead of 100 feet of strong rope, you have 190 feet of rope. Now you only have to rely on my thread for ten of the 200 feet. You can cross the chasm now, can't you? No? You mean you still don't feel safe to cross?

Okay, let's change the scenario once again. Instead of 190 feet of rope, you have 199 feet, 11 inches of good, stout rope. Now, there's only *one little inch* of thread in that entire span. Surely you can trust it now. Surely you can make the crossing of the chasm in complete confidence. No? Well, why not?

Because rope plus thread cannot save you! It must be good, stout rope all the way across or it cannot support you. And it is the same story with faith and works. Only faith in Christ is strong enough to support you. Faith plus works cannot save you. Your salvation cannot be 50 percent Christ and 50 percent you. It can't be 60/40 or 75/25 or even 99.99/.01. Christ must be your entire support, your entire salvation.

Charles Haddon Spurgeon put it this way: "If we had to put one stitch in the garment of our salvation, we would ruin the whole thing."

And so it is. We can't add anything to what Christ has already done. He has done it all!

Suppose a master wood craftsman builds a magnificent coffee table as a gift for a friend. He lavishes more loving care on this piece than on anything he has ever made. Over a six-month period, he hand-carves, hand-inlays, and hand-finishes the piece to perfection. Then he wraps it in a soft blanket to protect it, and he takes it to his friend's house. There, the craftsman presents the table with pride, an exquisite show-piece, spectacularly beautiful, lacking nothing.

"It's all yours," says the craftsman. "I made it for you because of our friendship, because of the love I have for you."

The other man is taken aback. "Oh!" he says. "It's the most beauti-ful thing I've ever seen!"

"You really like it?"

"Like it? I love it!" The man walks around it, admiring the gift from every angle. "It's too bad you had to do that whole table without any help, though . . . I know what! I'll get my belt sander out of the garage and put some finishing touches on it for you!"

Horrified, the craftsman jumps in front of the table to defend it. "Belt sander! Oh no, you don't! I won't let you within a mile of that table with your ten thumbs and your belt sander! You'll ruin the table! Don't you understand? It's finished!"

And so is our salvation. It is finished.

God is the master craftsman of our salvation. He needs no help from us. If you put your fingerprints on the salvation of God, which He crafted through Jesus Christ, you will ruin the whole thing.

Remember what Jesus said on the Cross? Remember the words He spoke just before He commended His spirit to the Father? That's right. He said, "It is almost finished."

What's that? Didn't I quote Him correctly? You mean, He didn't say "almost"? You know, I believe you're right! He said, "It is finished," period. In Greek, He said, "*Tetelestai!*"—the debt of sin has been paid in full!

When He gave His life upon the Cross, when He drank the cup of sin and wrath to the dregs, it wasn't *almost* finished. It wasn't finished except for the addition of our good works. It was totally, completely finished, period. The work of salvation has been fully accomplished. There is nothing any human being can add to it.

We are saved by Christ alone through faith alone. But faith is not mere belief, not mere mental assent to a set of doctrines and creeds. Authentic faith is never static. It is dynamic and active and alive. Authentic faith compels a believer to be continually engaged in good works. Being energized by the power of the Spirit of God, our faith cannot stand idle. The Spirit of the Living God has come to live in us, and we must be about our Father's business.

FREE!

Frank Barker was a jet pilot stationed at Pensacola, Florida, several decades ago. He was not the kind of man who gave much thought to God and matters of eternity. Late one Sunday night, after partying in some little town up the coast, he was returning to the base, trying to get back in time for reveille. He was used to flying fast, driving fast, and living fast, and on this particular night he was doing close to 90 miles per hour down one of those long, straight roads along the Florida panhandle that seem to go on forever.

As the miles flashed by, he was soon lulled to sleep by road hypnosis. The car veered off the road, and he awoke to see that his car was barreling through the forest. Panicked, he jammed on the brakes, but he was going so fast that he knew death was just a split second away. The car bounced over rutted earth. Tree branches flailed at his windshield. The brakes finally grabbed and the car skidded to a stop, tossing Frank over the steering wheel, then throwing him back onto the seat in a heap.

At first, he could hardly believe he was still alive. He peered out of the windshield and saw that his car had come to rest with its front bumper a scant two inches from the trunk of a massive tree. The head-lights illuminated a sign someone had nailed to the tree. It read: "The wages of sin is death."

Frank Barker thought he had received a personalized telegram from God. He got the message.

As he climbed out of the car, he was shaking so badly that he could hardly stand or walk. When he finally stopped shaking, he made his way back to the airbase and went to the chaplain's office. He told the chaplain he wanted to resign his commission and enter the ministry. So he did.

I became personally acquainted with Frank Barker when he attended Columbia Seminary. He was one of my classmates. I can still picture Frank sitting in the back row, leaning back against the wall with the most dumbfounded look on his face. He didn't have the faintest idea what the Christian faith or Christian theology or Christian history were all about—because he wasn't a Christian—yet! He was training to become a pastor, yet he hadn't even discovered the truth of the Christian faith.

All Frank Barker knew was that God had reached down, grabbed him by the scruff of the neck, and confronted him with the fact that "The wages of sin is death." He had learned part of the truth, but he still had to learn the "rest of the story" before he could become an authentic Christian and an effective pastor. Fortunately, he did and became a terrific pastor.

The statement from the Bible that so profoundly impacted Frank Barker is the bad-news half of one of those classic "good news, bad news" scenarios : "I have some good news and some bad news—which do you want to hear first?" In the Bible verse that so impacted Frank's life, God began with the bad news: "The wages of sin is death."

A man once said to me, "I know there's a verse in the Bible that says, 'The wages of sin is death.'" To which I replied, "No, there's no such verse in the Bible." With a shocked look on his face, he said, "Oh, I'm quite sure there is such a verse. I don't know the reference, but I know the verse is there—'The wages of sin is death.' I think it's in the New Testament somewhere."

"No," I said. "I can state with absolute certainty that no such verse exists."

At this point you may be a little puzzled. Like that man, you may be absolutely convinced that there is a Bible verse that says, "The wages of sin is death." You may even know the Scripture reference that eluded my friend: Romans 6:23. But it is not correct to say that the text of that verse is, "The wages of sin is death." That is only half the verse. That is just the bad news. The full text of that verse (emphasis added) is:

> For the wages of sin is death; but the *gift of God* is eternal life through
> Jesus Christ our Lord.

I've talked to many people over the years about that verse, and I find it amazing that, for some strange reason, the majority of people who are familiar with it only remember the bad news. They can't seem to remember the Good News: "The gift of God is eternal life through Jesus Christ our Lord." Isn't that astonishing? People generally remember good news and repress the bad. It is as if Satan has succeeded in blinding people's eyes to the glad tidings of the Gospel! We must always remember that there are spiritual forces doing their best to keep us from grasping what is essentially a simple concept: *Salvation is a free gift from God.* Heaven is free! That fundamental truth is at the heart of the Gospel of Jesus Christ. That is why Satan continually tries to prevent us from understanding it.

Don't ever forget the Good News: Salvation is *free.*

Every once in a while you will see a sign that says, "Free!" How do you react to such a sign? Do you instantly believe it, or do your inner defenses go up? Most of us think, *What's the catch?* There is an old maxim that says, "If it looks too good to be true, it probably is." And all of that is perfectly true in our material world, in our economic system, in our social system. If somebody offers you something for nothing, always look for the hook.

But in the spiritual world, the world of the things of God, the opposite is true. In God's economy, there is nothing that you can purchase—which is just as well, since you have no currency that is any good in God's Heaven. What God offers you as a free gift, no strings attached, you could not afford to buy if it were for sale and you wanted it desperately. God is not a salesman. He has nothing to sell. The Church has nothing to sell. The Bible has nothing to sell. Salvation is free.

Someone once said, "The problem with most Christians is not that they can't sell the Gospel; they can't even *give* it away!" I've seen the truth of that statement myself. We as Christians have not only the Good News, but the Best News the world has ever heard. Yet, when we share that news with people, they often respond with an argument or a curse or an uninterested shrug and a cold shoulder. Why is that?

Perhaps, to some degree, it's because people just can't accept the simple truth that salvation is *free.* They think that Heaven *must be* a reward, it *must be* something we earn, it *must be* something that is deserved, merited, worked for, and achieved by our own effort and goodness. The idea that salvation is simply a gift that we reach out and accept seems *wrong* to our wary, suspicious minds. *You don't get something for nothing,* we think. *There's got to be a catch.*

I am reminded of the story (purely fictional, of course) about a man who died and went to Heaven. There he was greeted by Peter, who said, "You want to get into Heaven? Okay, here's how we play the game. You tell me some of the good things you've done, and I'll tell you how many points you get for each one. If you get a hundred points, you get in."

"Okay," said the man, a little dubiously. "I think I understand." He had never heard before that there was a game for getting into Heaven.

"All right," said Peter. "Now, tell me: What good things have you done?"

"Well," said the man, thinking back over his life, "I've lived with one woman for fifty years and have never been unfaithful."

"Marvelous!" said Peter. "That's two points."

"Only two points?" said the man, his brow furrowing in concern.

"Boy, this is going to be tougher than I thought." He reflected some more, then said, "Well, I went to church every week and never missed a Sunday. I went to Sunday school, too. I have perfect attendance pins that go all the way down to my knee."

"Excellent," said Peter. "Very good. That's three points."

Now the man was beginning to perspire. "Oh, and I wanted to help other people," he said hopefully, "so I opened a soup kitchen for the poor. I was there feeding poor people every Saturday for more than thirty years."

"Oh, that's very good," said Peter. "That's another three points."

At this point, the man got exasperated. "That's all? Just three lousy points? Why, at this rate, it's going to take the grace of God Himself to get me through those gates!"

"Bingo!" said Peter. "One hundred points. Come on in."

And there it is, my friend. Heaven is *free*! And why is it free? That is what grace is all about—totally unmerited, undeserved, unearned favor from God.

Grace *had* to be free. Salvation *had* to be a gift. Why? Because we have nothing to pay with. We are spiritually impoverished—as impoverished as that man who stood at the gates of Heaven. All have sinned, and the wages of sin is death. On every page, in every paragraph of the book of our lives, there is an ugly black smudge of sin—some evil thought or word or deed or omission or commission. Any one of those smudges of sin is enough, all by itself, to bar us from the gates of heaven. Only grace could let us through those gates. A free gift is the only kind of salvation we could ever afford.

The great golfer Arnold Palmer was once invited to go to Saudi Arabia, where he played a series of golf matches. At the end of the series, the Saudi king, who was a golf fan, said that he admired Palmer's abilities and wanted to give him a gift by which to remember his time in the Saudi state.

Palmer smiled and demurred, "No, thank you. I really don't want any gifts. It was my pleasure to be here."

But the king insisted. "I must do something for you. Just name it—whatever you want."

"All right," said Palmer, "I guess you could give me a golf club. That would be a nice memento." He was thinking he could have the club inscribed, and he could display it in his den with his other trophies and keepsakes.

The next day one of the king's officials showed up at Palmer's hotel to present him with the gift: the deed to a golf club. Not a shaft with a handgrip at one end and a head at the other, but a piece of real estate with greens, fairways, bunkers, lakes, and a clubhouse—all eighteen holes!

The moral to this story is clear: Never ask for anything small when you are in the presence of a king!

When we begin to understand the grace we have received, the free gift of everlasting life that is ours simply for the taking, it is inevitable that we fall in love with Christ. That, truly, is what a Christian is—someone who is in love with Christ.

I was trying to explain to a man that salvation is truly free, but he could not grasp the simplicity of this truth. He kept saying, "But that can't be all there is to it! Certainly, I have to do *something* in order to earn eternal life. It can't simply be free!"

So I said to him, "Do you know what I did last week to earn eternal life?"

"No," he said, "please tell me."

"Absolutely nothing," I said. "And do you know what I plan to do next week to gain eternal life?"

"What?"

"Nothing. I didn't do anything last year to get eternal life. In fact, I haven't done one thing in my entire life to get eternal life. And I don't plan to ever do one single thing to get eternal life. Why? Because I already have it. More than forty years ago, eternal life was given to me as a gift."

He pondered that for a moment, and I added, "Of course, this last week I did try to show my gratitude to Christ for giving me that gift. And this week I also plan to try to show my gratitude and love to Christ for what He has done for me. But I don't plan to do anything to try to *gain* eternal life, because Christianity is not about *trying;* it's about *trusting.* If you want eternal life, you have to *stop trying,* my friend, and *start trusting* in Jesus Christ."

Are you trying to earn your way to Heaven? If so, stop! The only thing you can earn for all eternity is death. That's the bad news: The wages of sin is death. We are all sinners, and if we get what we earn, we collect a paycheck of death—physical death, spiritual death, eternal death. But now the Good News: The free, unearned, gracious gift of God is eternal life, paid for in full by Jesus Christ.

For years, I had a savior named Jim Kennedy. I was in the savior business, trying to save myself—but the business was a complete failure. Finally, I recognized my own poverty, filed for spiritual bankruptcy, got out of the savior business, and put my trust in the only Savior worthy of the name, Jesus Christ. I recommend Him to you.

I would stop there, but I must add one postscript:

The offer of the free gift of eternal life may be recalled at any time. I cannot promise you that it will be available tomorrow or next week. At any moment, the day of grace may suddenly and irrevocably end, and Christ may appear. On that day, the offer will be forever recalled.

So if you have never received that free gift, why wait one minute longer?

Now is the accepted time. Today is the day of salvation!

NOTES

Mystery 2: Is It Possible Not to Sin?
1. From "Blessed Assurance," by Fanny J. Crosby (1820–1915).

Mystery 4: Should We Judge or Not Judge?
1. Shavahn Dorris, "Don't Be a Closet Christian," *Dallas Morning News*, 19 September 1999, 7J.

Mystery 5: The Mystery of the Virgin Birth
1. Electronically retrieved from http://religion.rutgers.edu/jseminar/.
2. Information on the Jesus Seminar was taken from these sources: Larry Witham, "Evangelists Dispute Revisionist View of a Radical Christ," *The Washington Times*, 7 August 1995, 23; Robert L. Wilken, "The Real Jesus: The Misguided Quest for the Historical Jesus and the Truth of the Traditional Gospels," *Commonweal*, 8 March 1996, 19-20; Larry David McCormick, "Scholarly Skeptics Remake Jesus on Their Own Terms," *The Bergen Record*, 21 October 1999, H12; Ted Byfield, "The Jesus Seminar was a Fraud and a Scam Which Easily Sucked In the Gullible Media," *Alberta Report / Western Report*, 3 June 1996, 34; Jeffery L. Sheler, "Bob Funk's Radical Reformation Roadshow," *U.S. News & World Report*, 4 August 1997, 55; Nancy Gibbs, "Cover Story: The Message of Miracles—As the Faithful Hunger for Them, Scholars Rush to Debunk and to Doubt," *Time*, 10 April 1995, 64ff; David Van Biema, "Religion: The Gospel Truth?—The Iconoclastic and Provocative Jesus Seminar Argues That Not Much of the New Testament Can Be Trusted," *Time*, 8 April 1996, 52ff.
3. Josh McDowell, *The New Evidence That Demands a Verdict* (Nashville: Thomas Nelson, 1999), 34; "Homer," *Columbia Encyclopedia*, Fifth Edition (New York: Columbia University Press, 1993), electronically retrieved at http://www.elibrary.com.
4. Quoted by McDowell, *The New Evidence That Demands a Verdict*, 46.
5. Jeffrey Hadden, results of a survey of 7,441 Protestant ministers published in *PrayerNet Newsletter*, 13 November 1998, 1.

Mystery 6: More Mysteries of the Birth of Christ: Genealogies and Prophecies

1. Dan Barker, "A Myth," *Capital Times* (Madison, WI), 20 December 1993, 1C.
2. The Palestinian (Jerusalem) Talmud, Sanhedrin, folio 24, cited by Chuck Missler in "Until Shiloh Comes," http://www.yfiles.com/shiloh.html.
3. Augustin Lemann, *Jesus Before the Sanhedrin* (1886, translated by Julius Magath), cited by Chuck Missler in "Until Shiloh Comes," http://www.yfiles.com/shiloh.html.

Mystery 7: Mysteries of the Death and Resurrection of Christ

1. Jeff Lowder, "The Historicity of Jesus' Resurrection," electronically retrieved at http://www.infidels.org/library/modern/jeff_lowder/jesus_resurrection/ chap3.html; Jim Leffel, "Basic Christianity, Week Four: Why Should I Look to the Bible, Anyway?" electronically retrieved at http://www.xeons.org/classes/bcweek4.htm; Peter J. Leithart, "Testing the Modernity Thesis," *Premise*, vol. 2, no. 3, 27 March 1995, 4, electronically retrieved at http://capo.org/premise/95/march/lmodern.html.
2. McDowell, *The New Evidence That Demands a Verdict*, 38, 66–67.

Mystery 8: Doesn't the Genesis Creation Story Contradict Science?

1. Clifton Fadiman, ed., *The Little, Brown Book of Anecdotes* (Boston: Little, Brown and Co., 1985), 343.
2. Michael Denton, *Evolution: A Theory in Crisis* (Bethesda, MD: Adler & Adler, 1996).
3. Stephen Jay Gould, "The Evolution of Life on Earth," *Scientific American*, October 1994, electronically retrieved at http://www.geocities.com/ CapeCanaveral/Lab/2948/gould.html.
4. Frank Zindler, in a debate with William Lane Craig, *Atheism vs. Christianity*, Zondervan Video, 1996.
5. Sir Arthur Keith, *Evolution and Ethics* (New York: G. P. Putnam's Sons, 1947), 230.
6. J. Tenenbaum, *Race and Reich* (New York: Twayne Publications, 1956), 211.
7. Quoted by David T. Moore, *Five Lies of the Century: How Many Do You Believe?* (Wheaton, IL: Tyndale House, 1995), 114.
8. David N. Menton, Ph.D., "The Religion of Nature: Social Darwinism," originally published in *St. Louis MetroVoice*, September 1994, electronically retrieved at http://www.gennet.org/metro15.htm.
9. Keith, *Evolution and Ethics*, 230.
10. John Gribbin and Jeremy Cherfas, *The Monkey Puzzle* (New York: Pantheon, 1982), 31.
11. Quoted on a Web page about Adam Sedgwick, electronically retrieved at http://www.ucmp.berkely.edu/history/sedgwick.html.

Mystery 9: Doesn't the Book of Genesis Contradict Itself?

1. Peter Sparrow, "The Creation Bus . . . and Us," electronically retrieved at http://www.answersingenesis.org/docs/3137.asp.

Mystery 10: The Mystery of the Incarnation: Is Jesus God—or the Son of God?

1. C. S. Lewis, *Mere Christianity* (New York: Touchstone/Simon & Schuster, 1996 ed.), 55.
2. Ibid., p. 56.
3. Walter C. Erdman, *More Sources of Power in Famous Lives* (Nashville: Cokesbury Press, 1937), 116–117.
4. McDowell, *The New Evidence That Demands a Verdict*, 161.

Mystery 11: The Mystery of the Trinity: How Can God Be Both *Three* and *One*?

1. Words by Thomas Ken (1637–1711); public domain.

Mystery 12: How Can a Loving God Send People to Hell?

1. Clifton Fadiman, ed., *The Little, Brown Book of Anecdotes*, 207–208.
2. From "The Spacious Firmament," words by Joseph Addison, music by Joseph Haydn; public domain.

Mystery 13: Are We Saved by Faith or by Works?

1. A. W. Tozer, "Antinomianism," article electronically retrieved at http://www.blessedhope.simplenet.com/tozer25.htm.

ABOUT THE AUTHOR

DR. D. JAMES KENNEDY is the senior minister of Coral Ridge Presbyterian Church in Fort Lauderdale, Florida, a church with nearly ten thousand members. He is founder and president of Evangelism Explosion International, the first ministry to be established in every nation on earth. Dr. Kennedy is also chancellor of Knox Theological Seminary; founder of the Center for Christian Statesmanship in Washington, D.C. (which endeavors to bring the Gospel of Christ to those who hold the reins of power in our government); and founder of the Center for Reclaiming America (which seeks to equip men and women to work in their communities to transform our culture). He is the author of more than forty books.

Dr. Kennedy's messages are broadcast by television and radio to more than forty thousand cities and towns in America and 156 foreign countries, making him the most-listened-to Presbyterian minister in the world.

Dr. Kennedy is a *summa cum laude* graduate and holds nine degrees, including the Ph.D. He is listed in several dozen registries, including *2000 Outstanding Intellectuals of the 20th Century, International Man of the Year 1999–2000,* and *1000 Leaders of World Influence.*

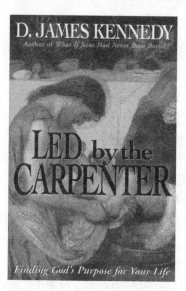